Praise for *Born Just Right*

"Infectious . . . An affirmation that, with support and resources, kids with disabilities can shine—or sparkle."
—*Kirkus Reviews*c"A realistic picture of the feelings that accompany being different."

—*SLJ*

"An inspiring memoir for any collection."
—*Booklist*

BORN just RIGHT

JORDAN REEVES & JEN LEE REEVES

JETER CHILDREN'S

ALADDIN

New York London Toronto Sydney New Delhi

ALADDIN

An imprint of Simon & Schuster Children's Publishing Division

1230 Avenue of the Americas, New York, New York 10020

First Aladdin paperback edition June 2020

Text copyright © 2019 by Jennifer Lee Reeves

Cover photograph copyright © 2020 by Amy Enderle

Cover hand-lettering copyright © 2020 by Jenna Stempel-Lobell

Interior photographs courtesy of the Reeves family

Also available in an Aladdin hardcover edition.

All rights reserved, including the right of reproduction in whole or in part in any form.

ALADDIN and related logo are registered trademarks of Simon & Schuster, Inc.

For information about special discounts for bulk purchases, please contact Simon & Schuster Special Sales at 1-866-506-1949 or business@simonandschuster.com.

The Simon & Schuster Speakers Bureau can bring authors to your live event. For more information or to book an event contact the Simon & Schuster Speakers Bureau at 1-866-248-3049 or visit our website at www.simonspeakers.com.

Designed by Heather Palisi

The text of this book was set in Adobe Caslon Pro.

Manufactured in the United States of America 0520 OFF

2 4 6 8 10 9 7 5 3 1

The Library of Congress has cataloged the hardcover edition as follows:

Names: Reeves, Jen Lee, author.

Title: Born just right / by Jen Lee Reeves and Jordan Reeves.

Description: New York : Aladdin/Jeter Publishing, 2019. | Audience: Age 9–13. |

Identifiers: LCCN 2018051714 (print) | LCCN 2018059915 (eBook) |

ISBN 9781534428409 (eBook) | ISBN 9781534428386 (hc) |

Subjects: LCSH: Reeves, Jordan—Health. | Artificial arms—Patients—United States—Biography—Juvenile literature. | Arm—Abnormalities—Patients—United States—Biography—Juvenile literature.

Classification: LCC RD756.2 (eBook) | LCC RD756.2 .R44 2019 (print) |

DDC 617.5/74—dc23

LC record available at https://lccn.loc.gov/2018051714

ISBN 9781534428393 (pbk)

To every person who helped us grow and learn . . .
especially Dad and Cameron
and everyone who was born just right

CONTENTS

INTRODUCTION

If you could be any type of superhero, what would you become?

My name is Jordan, and that question took me in directions I never could have imagined.

That's because when I had the chance to become a superhero, I became a brand-new one . . . a hero who could look beyond my physical difference and use it to my advantage. I discovered a fun project that gave me my own kind of superpowers. I found a way to combine glitter and 3-D printing to create something so fun, even someone who doesn't like glitter will smile. (My mom was never a glitter fan, but she lightened up a lot.)

I always say there are too many books about physical differences and not enough stories that just happen to include a person with a physical difference.

This book is about me. I was born with one full arm and one short arm that stopped growing just above the elbow. And my story is about pushing beyond what's "normal." It has adventure, creativity, and lots of *glitter*. My limb difference doesn't define me, but it has given me so many opportunities to see the world in a different way.

I've had a chance to meet so many amazing people and travel to different parts of the country, learning about the disability world and so much more. I've learned to be physically and mentally strong, thanks to years of occupational and physical therapy, but also because of sports and other activities! I've attended an amazing summer camp for kids with limb differences since I was three years old. I've also had the chance to meet kids across the country through a website my mom launched when

I was a baby. It's called Born Just Right because my family always says I'm "just right," and I was born with "just" a right hand! (That usually makes people giggle when they hear that play on words.)

I've also learned how powerful I can be, especially when it comes to thinking outside the box and introducing my ideas to the world. I believe I can do just about anything (other than monkey bars), and so can you!

1
BORN JUST RIGHT: MY BEGINNINGS

My parents didn't know I had a limb difference before I was born on December 29, 2005. Doctors say the circulation in my arm didn't work properly while I was growing. That's why I was born with a left arm that stopped just above the elbow. I've never known a life with two hands or two elbows, so it seems totally normal to live a one-handed life.

My birth story is pretty sweet. Mom says she noticed I was born without a hand before anyone else in the room. She asked if I was okay, and the doctor said I was fine. Mom looked up at my dad, and they both agreed. My parents had never even *seen* a person with one hand until they met me. What's cool is that they didn't freak out about it. Just like the doctor said, they knew I was fine. My family has never treated me any different from how they treat my older brother, Cameron. Instead, they have all encouraged me to *figure it all out*.

Which is a good thing. That's because I'm pretty stubborn. I like to take care of things myself! For example, I learned how to put on my socks and shoes when I was really young, in preschool. I remember one time I was in a toddler dance class and all the other kids needed their parents' help. I shocked everyone when I sat on the floor and shouted, "I DO IT!" I stuck my toes into my socks and worked my feet in with one hand. I might have been a little slower, but I didn't need or want help!

That stubbornness gets me in trouble sometimes, but I think it's also why I can think up ideas to solve a problem that might be easier for someone with two hands. There aren't a lot of people around me who have one hand, so I often have to figure out two-handed things my own way. That usually means trying and trying different ways until I find the one that works. Besides putting on my own shoes and socks, zippers and buttons were also tricky for me when I was little. I learned quickly that even though I might have failed at my first attempt, if I kept trying, I would eventually find the answer. I feel lucky my family didn't step in and do it all for me, or else I probably wouldn't have so many big ideas! My parents say they would have to bite their tongues to keep from offering help sometimes when I was little. They knew I could figure out a lot of things just by having enough time to solve a problem. I walked when I was ready to walk. I had my own technique for putting on clothes and shoes. I didn't always learn those skills at the same pace as kids with typical bodies, but since my parents didn't do things for me, I found my own way. They were teaching me how to be a problem-solver without even realizing it!

I went to a day care center when I was a baby and moved to a preschool when I was a little older. I was the only one-handed kid anyone had ever met. But we were growing up together and learning things together. I didn't get teased because the kids were used to me. And there's something about little kids. They seem to get used to someone who looks different faster than older kids do. But no matter what age I am, there are some things that take me longer to learn. In preschool, that was super obvious. My teachers didn't know how to give me one-handed tips. I did have a therapist who came to school to help me work on those tricky things that we call "life skills."

Life skills are also challenging when it comes to meeting new people. I attend public school, and that means I meet new people all the time. When I started in kindergarten, kids weren't used to me. My mom made a little picture book that the teachers would read at the start of the school year that showed off all the things I can do. We showed a different version of the book every year until fifth grade. It was a really easy way for kids to see for themselves how I could do a lot of cool things. The book also helped kids know that they had to ask before they touched my little arm. It looks different, so some kids think it's a great idea to grab it and see what it feels like. The problem is, I don't like being grabbed. (Who does?) The book helped kids feel comfortable around me *and* taught them to respect my personal space.

These days, I really don't like that book. I know it helped, but that book just reminds me of the harder times when kids weren't used to having me around school. As the years went on, I made more and more friends. They learned that just because I'm different, that doesn't mean I'm scary. I can still be a really good friend. I don't plan to do anything special to introduce my difference when I start middle school, or even when I start high school. People are going to figure out I'm okay just by getting to know me first.

A little book didn't stop all my problems at school. There were mean kids on the playground. (I wasn't afraid to complain about them to my principal.) There were kids who would whisper or stare as I walked by in the hallway. I had strange experiences in my after-school program. But most of the time, the kids would learn how my disability might look different but that I didn't let it stop me from doing my best.

MY FAMILY

My family is a big part of my life. My dad is a journalist who runs a television newsroom. He also teaches at a university. My mom also works at the same university, and she does cool work on websites and helps different organizations. My brother, Cameron, is four years older than I am, and I think I can do pretty much everything he can do. Actually, I think I can do *more* than he can. My parents are always reminding me that I'm younger, and that drives me crazy. I really don't consider us to be that different.

Cameron has always wanted to help me. Growing up, my mom had to remind him to let me figure things out and do it my own way. The story Mom always uses as an example is a time when we had a homemade sandbox in our backyard. It had a wood side that I needed to climb over to get into the sand. For some reason, that wasn't really easy for me to do. My mom says she remembers physically holding my brother back to keep him from helping me into the sandbox. She wanted me to find a way to get in all by myself. My brother tells me that it made him super angry. He always wanted to help when I was small. I think he still does at times. That's probably why he and I butt heads often. We both think we can do everything better than the other.

I grew up (and still live) in Columbia, a small city in Missouri. We live in a house that is kind of magical. That's because it is next to a small lake that gives us a chance to enjoy swimming in the summer and beautiful sunsets all year. I love sitting on our dock and dangling my feet into the water. There are lots of fish and ducks and geese that hang out around the lake too. It's just so peaceful. I think my bedroom has the best view of all the rooms in our house. I can sit on my floor, read books, and stare out at the lake forever. I am so lucky to have a home that feels peaceful, even if my mom and dad are always trying to get me to keep it clean!

I have grown up with dogs in the house. These days, we have a huge black goldendoodle named Bailey and a gray Weimaraner mix named Blue. I think they are the best dogs in the world. I love cuddling with them when they aren't running around playing catch or barking at dogs or other animals. They are a big part of my family too.

We don't live close to any other family members, and we only get to see them for a little bit each year, so the four of us do a lot together. We do a lot of traveling. My family also goes to football games, basketball games, and music shows together. We have college football season tickets, and that gives us an excuse to tailgate a lot in the fall. Tailgates are when my parents set up a tent and a grill near a parking lot before football games. We hang out there for hours before going to the football stadium. We get to see all kinds of my parents' friends. I even get to have my friends join me sometimes. We also have a lot of fun with everyone when there are big music festivals or when we want to have a lot of people over to our house.

These days, my parents also go to a lot of my and Cameron's activities. I used to dance a lot. Recently, I was involved in sports, including cross-country, track, softball, and basketball. I take piano and voice lessons. I am also part of a Girl Scout troop. I love trying everything out to see what I like. I guess I'm still figuring out my favorite activities. I don't feel like I have to pick and choose just yet.

DYNAMIC DUO: A NOTE FROM JORDAN'S MOM, JEN

Jordan has always sparkled. Even before she started shooting glitter. People would walk up to her when she was a baby and notice a little extra shine in her eyes. It's like she was always ready to change perceptions from the start.

Jordan and I are a team. I'm also her mom, so I have to do mom things (like say no sometimes). But we also have a relationship that is a little different because we travel and experience so many things together. First, we were together all the time when she was a baby. I didn't know what extra things I needed to do for her when she was born, so I took her to a lot of doctors' appointments. We traveled out of state often to build prosthetics starting when she was ten months old. We attended extra summer camps and events for kids with limb differences starting when Jordan was three. Her brother, Cameron, is four years older, and he got to come along with us sometimes. Their dad (my husband) would attend these events when he could. (My jobs have been a little more flexible through the years.)

I gave Jordan space to find solutions to her challenges. Maybe it's because I talked to so many other parents of limb-different kids. I knew that I needed to step back and give her room to learn. That's really hard when you see someone you love struggle. But giving her the chance to discover solutions has also given her brain the space to think up different ideas and have very strong opinions of her own. Yes, that means there are times when we argue. But I often realize she's a lot like me: strong-willed, confident, and willing to take a stand on issues that matter.

When Jordan was a baby, I worried about what she couldn't do. I had never experienced the world outside a typically formed body. Every time she figured out a new task, I felt a little less worried. These days, I never assume there is a "can't" in Jordan's world. She can do it all, with or without a prosthetic arm helping her out.

I used to be a journalist, and I documented my experiences with Jordan as she's grown up in an online blog. That gave us more opportunities to talk to and meet kids and families across the country, and even around the world! It's a gift to get to know so many people and learn from their life experiences. While Jordan and I can share the lessons we've learned through the years, it's exciting to learn from everyone else at the same time.

Watching Jordan speak up for issues that matter to her was not something I expected as I've watched her grow. But she and I both committed to each other that we would do what we can to help others who may not have the same opportunities that have come Jordan's way. I am proud to be by her side as she shares her thoughts and opinions of the disability world. We wouldn't be on this adventure if she wasn't in the lead.

WRITING EVERYTHING ONLINE

When I was younger, my mom wrote a blog about me. That might sound a little creepy, but it helped me meet a lot of amazing people and go places I never would have gone. She says she was reporting about our lives so we could help parents of limb-different kids. As my parents figured out what I needed to be healthy and confident, others got to use our experiences as a resource.

I haven't read all of my mom's posts. I know she didn't always know how to help me when I was little. She spent a lot of time asking a lot of questions to other parents, doctors, and therapists. She and my dad learned that the best way to help me succeed was by encouraging me to try new things instead of coming up with solutions for me. My mom wrote how she thought it was a good thing I was so cute, because I was so stubborn, it drove her crazy. It took me years to figure out how to tie my shoes. One day, it just clicked. I had tried so many different ways, but then it finally made sense to me. I use a combination of my hand and my little arm to get it done. I wouldn't let my mom help me with putting on my clothes. I had to figure out how to get the toothpaste on the toothbrush. I was going to put that seat belt on, darn it! I'm really glad my parents gave me room to learn, even if I made it hard on them. My mom told me there were a ton of things she and my dad didn't think I could do when I was born. But she never told me her doubts at the time. She only told me how she felt recently. I'm so glad she kept it to herself. If I'd known about the doubts, it might have made me less confident.

Two-handed people with typical bodies just don't understand what it's like to live with a physical disability. They assume everything we do each day needs the help of a traditional body. But think about it. A lot of things are possible if you shift your perspective. My perspective is one-handed. Nothing intimidates me. I like challenges. But I also like access to tools that can help me when I need them.

2
HELPER ARMS

Growing up was a little different for me. I got my first prosthetic arm when I was ten months old. I call prosthetics "helper arms." My first helper arm wasn't super easy to use, but it helped me build muscles. Strangely enough, that was just what I needed with that old arm. I was born with weakness in my neck and torso. That meant I had a hard time sitting up on my own. My first helper arm helped me get stronger. I have always traveled out of state to get prosthetics made. (My parents tried to build one with a company in my town, but

I grew out of it in a couple of weeks. My mom wasn't going to go through an experience like that again.)

I've used helper arms for most of my life. Today, my helper arms still make me stronger and help me do specific things like hold on to a bike handle or do push-ups.

They haven't been super "handy," but they have helped me stay healthy. Helper arms have also trained my body to know what it's like to have two hands. Think about your arms. If you have two shoulders, two elbows, and two hands, you probably don't pay a lot of attention to how they work. But if you watch how you move, you'll see that you move your elbows a lot more than your shoulders. I use my left shoulder like an elbow, so I sometimes overuse it. My prosthetics give my shoulder a break from all that extra work. My parents are constantly worried about me overusing my shoulder, which could cause other physical issues later on.

Besides the practical use, wearing prosthetics means I get a chance to show off my sense of fashion and design. Ever since I was little, I've had a chance to decide what kind of "skin" I want with my helper arms. I've worn a

Disney Princess arm, a Hello Kitty arm, and lots of others with pretty colors, including blues, greens, purples, and even a sparkly blue.

THERAPY

Even though I was determined to do things my way, some things were not easy for me when I was little. I took a really long time learning to walk. Instead, I would scoot around on my butt. I was really fast, but it wasn't the most efficient way to get around. My parents called me "Swiffer Butt" because I was always cleaning the floor as I moved, just like a mop. My body just needed to do things a little differently from some kids.

Up until I was in third grade, I saw a physical and occupational therapist every week. My therapists helped me build muscles and figure out tiny tasks that might be tricky with one hand (or tricky with one hand and a helper arm). Think about opening those milk cartons they sell at school. Or opening a juice pouch. Try opening a potato chip bag with one hand, without your teeth! (My mom doesn't like me opening anything with my teeth.) Those are just a few skills I would work on so I didn't need to ask for a lot of help in the school cafeteria.

All the hard work I did when I was little made it easier to participate in other activities, like soccer (which I don't like) and dancing (which I love!).

Now, I'm a really active kid, but prosthetics aren't helpful for me to wear all the time. They can feel like they're in the way or they don't really help with a specific activity. Since I can't—and don't want to—wear them all the time, physical therapy is a good way to keep an eye on any damage I might cause my body. I have to visit a physical therapist every once in a while to make sure I'm not causing serious damage. I know one-handed adults who needed major shoulder or wrist surgeries because they didn't listen to their bodies when things hurt from overuse. Outside of therapy, I try to work out with my sports and with weights when I have time to go to the gym. I learned a lot of adaptive workouts with a really great CrossFit Kids coach. I also try to follow some yoga and Pilates exercises. Keeping my core strong is a really great way to make sure I'm healthy.

Sometime during elementary school, I was seeing a physical therapist about shoulder pain when I mentioned I couldn't touch my toes. It hurt too much. It turns out, I wasn't walking properly. My therapist told me I was holding my little arm to my side and not moving it when I walked or ran. That started hurting the muscles in my legs. People tend to think that my little arm and prosthetic are specifically the only things that I have to strengthen and work on, but it actually has an effect on my entire body! I had to relearn how to walk and run! I really had to think about moving both of my arms to get my legs working the right way. Wearing my prosthetic arm was another way to help remind me that I needed to move my arms when I walked. It took a couple of months, but I always remember to move both sides of my body. And when I run now, I'm really fast.

BUT IT'S SO HARD, MOMMY: A NOTE FROM
JORDAN'S MOM, JEN
(FROM A 2013 BLOG POST; JORDAN WAS SEVEN)

For almost all eight years I've written this blog, I've focused on Jordan's health. Everything I do is focused on making sure she is strong mentally and physically. That's why we've made a glorious return to occupational therapy to prevent periodic shoulder pain. Our recent appointments have shown Jordan's left shoulder blade is weak and it could be to blame for some of her recent clavicle pain. Her shoulder also has some slight separation as well.

Jordan has *always* been a piece of work during occupational and physical therapy appointments. Always. She acts goofy, she half listens, she challenges the therapist to the core. It's a big reason why I worked with the same OT for most of Jordan's life. She figured out how to deal with Jordan most of the time. Our new therapist is managing all of those personality challenges without the history. We're trying really hard to make the most out of the hour we see her each week.

During this week's appointment, Jordan was introduced to four new yoga exercises. Initially she was really excited because I often talk about how yoga is great exercise. Now that the helper arm is back in play, we were able to work on some exercises that were really challenging. They hurt. The exercises required attention, focus, and using muscles in ways that hurt Jordan. Not end-of-the-world hurt, but enough that it wasn't fun. *Not. One. Bit.*

Trying to get Jordan to participate and learn the positions enough times for her and me to understand what was expected was a bit taxing. Jordan wanted to play, and working hard during therapy isn't fun.

But we did it. We survived another appointment.

As we drove away, I asked Jordan if she understood why we go to occupational therapy. She said she didn't know, even though we talked about it a few weeks ago. So I told her about limb-different teenagers and adults I've met who have chronic pain. Others I know deal with pain if they don't exercise often enough. I explained to Jordan that my goal as her mom is to help her learn ways to stay strong and do whatever we can to prevent her from hurting a lot. A little bit of work can stop a lot of hurt when she's older.

"But it's so hard, Mommy."

Oh, my heart. I know, baby. I reminded Jordan how a year ago, she couldn't even run a couple of blocks with me. But we've worked and worked and she ran a whole mile with me without stopping last week. It took effort and hard work, but it got easier. I promised her that it will continue to get easier.

That's when she asked me what I did when I had to do yoga when I was little. And I had to explain that I didn't have to do exercises like that when I was little. I have a different body . . . and I don't know what it's like to know that I have to work hard just to make sure I'm not in pain when I get older. But I promised her, and I mean this: I will be her cheerleader and helper every step of the way. This hard work will be worth it. It will.

BUILDING ARMS

I didn't realize all the therapy and helper-arm-building was teaching me about fit, function, and design. It also taught me to speak up and share my opinions when something doesn't feel right.

I learned a lot because of my prosthetist. I've worked with him since I was two years old. My mom traveled to a couple of different places with me as a baby to get my helper arms. After doing a lot of research, she discovered an expert in Chicago. That's when we started working with David Rotter, or Mr. David, as I call him. After working with him for so long, he feels like an extra family member to me.

Building helper arms is *work*. My mom and I usually block off a week so I can go into the office for a few days, test the designs out over the weekend, and then spend a few more days finishing the work before we go home. Most people build helper arms and legs over a number of different appointments that can last for weeks or even months.

Buying a prosthetic is not like buying new clothes or a coat. It's a lot more personal. It has to fit really well, and you want to feel confident when you wear it. I get to pick how mine looks. Each time we build a new arm, I can pick the color and the themes that go with it. I used to put characters on my prosthetic, but now I focus on cool patterns and sometimes extra sparkles.

We build a new arm every eighteen months or so. That's when my mom and I travel to Chicago. We work in a medical office that's in the basement of a city hospital. You have to check in with security guards and wait for a really slow elevator to get there. Each time, we get to work in an appointment room that's for little kids. Because we visit for an intense week of appointments, my mom and I set up shop in that room. I bring crafts and books, and my mom brings her work computer. We try to have fun and be silly as much as we can.

Beyond our appointment room, there's an area where other patients meet with Mr. David behind closed curtains. It's a long room where I've been known to ride my scooter. Sometimes, Mr. David introduces me to other people who are meeting with him. I've met other kids and adults with limb differences. But I also get to visit a special part of the office that not everyone gets to see . . . the fabrication room. That's where Mr. David and his team work on building legs and arms and other things that help people. There are all kinds of machines and tools. It kind of feels like a combination car-repair garage and craft room. There's also a big 3-D printer, a monster machine that takes a design on a computer and prints it out using really thin layers of plastic to form a real version of what's on the screen. The fabrication room is full of legs and arms in different areas. There are also stacks of types of fabric, plastic, and foam. You can even find leftover fabric from some of my old arms in the collection.

Everyone who works with patients in the office wears a medical coat. Other people sit in a small room at computers and work. It's not a very big space, but a lot gets done in that room. Since I've gotten older, Mr. David lets me come in and watch him work on my arm and other people's prosthetics. Last time, I even got to help him build my arm. I learn so much when I visit!

Building a helper arm is slow. But you want it to be slow, because if I don't get an arm that fits just right, I'm not going to wear it. Each appointment starts like the last. I get measured and then cast for my arm. Mr. David wraps my arm with fiberglass to get a perfect mold. That gives him the chance to design the arms around something that is shaped just like me. Using really special plastic, he can create a test socket. That's where he can make a test arm and I can decide if it's comfortable or not.

I am really picky about what I like when it comes to helper arms. I don't want my arm pinched, and I want the inside to be really smooth. Some of my arms have a harness that goes around my shoulder. That way, when I move my shoulder, the hand can open and close. The hands on my helper arm can look like hooks or even the shape of a hand. I don't really need them to look real. It's definitely more important that they help me with tasks. The hook hands have a way better grip than many of the prosthetic hands that look like real hands. There are times when I love having my arm look different. But there are other times when I just want to look like a two-handed person. If I could, I would rather just not wear anything. But when I need to, I want my prosthetics to feel good and look really cool. I've learned what I like by working with Mr. David through the years. As I've gotten older, I've gotten better at telling him what I like and don't like. Some of the things I like are arms that don't weigh a lot. The elbow and hands need to be easy to operate. I also like the inside of the arm to not feel super tight—but it needs to fit well enough that it won't slide off if I get sweaty. I can't tell you how many times I've had a prosthetic arm built to help me ride a bike slip off because I was so sweaty! That will get you strange looks on a bike trail!

On most of my visits to work with Mr. David, we stay with friends who live in downtown Chicago. That gives me the chance to experience city life. I don't really have a lot of public transportation where I live, so I love being able to go all over Chicago using the bus system and the trains. The last couple of visits, I've brought a scooter, so it's even easier to get around and explore.

Some of my favorite experiences in Chicago happen when I'm not at a Mr. David appointment. During one of my recent trips, I played at several different playgrounds and met so many great new friends. Playgrounds are a great place to meet other kids when you don't go to school in a city. The kids thought I lived in the city, and for some reason I thought that was really cool. I'm not afraid to admit I live somewhere small. But I also like knowing I can make friends anywhere, and they don't think I'm strange.

DAILY PROSTHETICS

Building my arms is a lot of fun. But when I get home, I have to use them. I know they help my body and they can sometimes help me with specific tasks, but it can feel like a burden. When I was younger, I would wear my arm to school every day and keep it on until lunch. That gave me time to balance out my body and give my shoulder a break from using it too much, but I would be able to take it off before I ate lunch or had other activities. There was one time I left my arm out on the playground. It was kind of embarrassing when someone had to return my arm to the classroom.

Have you ever looked at how your elbow moves? It doesn't just bend. It also turns. Prosthetic elbows can do the same thing, but they are really big and take up a lot of space. Since a prosthetic elbow is super big, it can't fit into prosthetics I wear. That's because my little arm is *too* long to fit a fancy elbow. The only kind that works is attaching hinges to give a bend. It isn't very natural because it can't rotate. It's kind of clunky and not super helpful. But I wear it a little every day because I know it helps my body. I also have specific hands that do specific tasks. My bike hand helps me hold on, and it also works really well with paddles when I canoe or kayak. I can do both without a helper arm. (But I'll admit, I'm not an awesome biker without a helper arm.)

For years I worked with therapists to use my arms better and to make sure my body was balanced. But these days, I only visit occupational or physical therapists when I have a specific pain or challenge. I focus more on sports and activities that keep me strong. No matter what, I know that using prosthetics my whole life has helped me stay healthy and learn a lot.

My parents never really needed to change the house around for my limb difference. I do have a few adaptive pieces of silverware to make it easier to cut food. (One looks like a tiny guillotine that chops food around a fork.) I also need a smaller keyboard for some tasks at school. When it comes to clothes, I don't get my sleeve altered—I just roll it up. We don't buy coats or shirts that don't roll up easily. It is always a bummer when I find something that looks really nice but doesn't roll. It's just little things that can be annoying with a little arm.

3
DON'T STARE, JUST ASK!

I have my moments. You know, when you wish things were different? Mine hit when I am feeling quiet. I'll admit, I have my hard times when I am tired of standing out in the crowd. I don't want to be the person teachers constantly pick out when we're all doing something wrong. I just want to melt into the background. But the older I get, the more I seem to stick out. I've had a chance to share my story, and that makes it really hard to hide. But there are still times when I just want to hide in my room, veg out, watch videos, and pretend nothing is happening in my world.

I cried about my little arm for the first time when I was almost four years old. Even though my mom says she felt sad, she wasn't going to stop me. She and my dad never tried to fix me—they knew they could only do their best to help me deal with all the challenges that would come my way. They have given me tools to help me, and some of those tools include lots of different hands. I'm grateful that my limb difference has offered me extra opportunities in my life. But sometimes I'd be okay if all the cool stuff would go away and I could hide and not be so different around everyone else. I think it's okay to be sad sometimes, but I never let it hang over me. I've learned I need to stop and keep going, keep trying. Being sad all the time isn't worth it.

I'm not saying everything in my life is easy. But I find new ways to power through tough days.

T-SHIRT POWER

One way I push back on the things that make me upset is to find clothes that help me feel stronger. It all started when I went to a new dance class filled mostly with kids I didn't know. During that first class, a couple of kids would not stop staring at me. They just kept looking and whispering to one another. It made me so angry and sad, especially since they weren't even bothering to try to talk to me directly.

I went home and talked to my mom about the kids. I was upset. I couldn't figure out a way to stop the staring and whispering. I usually have at least one friend around who can back me up and say something to kids who are rude. But in this case, I didn't feel like I had someone in that room who could help me. I also didn't know the dance teacher very well. When I don't have a friend to back me up, I sometimes will ask an adult to help. But I didn't feel right asking her this time. I just felt uncomfortable, without many options to feel better in the class the next week.

I have had the chance to talk to grown-ups who have limb differences, and they say you eventually just don't notice the stares. I know there are times when I don't see them either. But that just isn't the case for me all the time.

My mom and I talked it through, and we came up with a really great idea. What if I went to the next class wearing a shirt that said something about staring so others in the class knew how I felt? That's why I had a shirt made that said, DON'T STARE, JUST ASK.

I wore my DON'T STARE, JUST ASK shirt to the next dance class, and I don't know if it made a difference to the other kids. But I know I felt stronger. I've learned that when people stare, it isn't always a bad thing if they aren't being rude about it. It's natural to look at something you haven't seen before. If a person is watching me or my family while we are doing regular family stuff, then maybe that person can learn something. I really can do almost everything a two-handed person can do. I just might have to do it differently. If people are too shy or nervous to come up to me directly, I hope by watching me and my family, they won't need to stare next time. But I am much happier answering questions about my little arm than being around someone who is too uncomfortable to ask. I know not everyone feels that way when they look or sound different. But talking about differences makes me a lot more comfortable than whispers and staring. Plus, I hope I am able to help others learn about limb differences during these conversations.

★ ★ ★

My mom and I have created a bunch of other T-shirt designs to help me and other people feel a little stronger about our differences. Since I was really little, my mom has dressed me in a shirt that says DUDE, WHERE'S MY ARM? The shirt lets us know if someone is going to be a friend. If a person laughs at the shirt, they will be someone you want to hang out with. If they are uncomfortable with it, we don't have to hang out, and I've learned that their being uncomfortable is not something I can control.

My favorite shirt we created is a drawing of horses and one unicorn. It's a picture based on a story a mom commented about on Born Just Right. She says she tells her kids, "If you were looking out at a pasture full of horses and you noticed a unicorn, would you stop and look? Of course I would! I'd love to look at a unicorn. Well, kids with physical differences are unicorns. We stand out!" The shirt says CELEBRATE THE UNICORNS. I know I celebrate them every day. That shirt is probably why I love unicorns so much. They make me smile and feel strong.

BASEBALL FIELD PARENTS

Another way I try to change how people think about limb differences is by talking to grown-ups. I started getting good at it, thanks to all of Cameron's baseball games. Like a lot of little brothers and sisters, I had to go to all of his games. I wouldn't just sit in the stands and watch him play. I would hang out with my friends! During almost every game, there would be a younger kid who would come up to me and ask why I have one hand. Most of the time, I would be in a good mood and tell the kids how I was born this way. Most kids are okay with that explanation and move on. There are always one or two kids who just can't imagine that what I'm telling them is true. I usually don't think the questions are annoying. Remember—don't stare, just ask! I really like it when kids ask questions. It just sometimes takes a longer explanation. Often, I've used the movie *Finding Nemo* as a way to talk about my limb difference to kids who don't understand. In the movie, Nemo has a "lucky fin" that is smaller than his other fins. He's able to do everything in the movie. That little clown fish is a great way to tell kids how I'm okay, just like him.

What I don't like is when a parent will rush up to me and apologize for their kid's questions. I usually tell the parents that I *like* questions and I don't think it's a problem at all. I hope more parents talk to their kids and let them know that not every kid is born looking like a traditional person. Lots of people have physical differences. One way a person can be different is that they may not have hands or feet! If this was a conversation everyone had with kids, people would stare less!

Beyond talking to adults one at a time, I got to speak about staring and my thoughts on disability during a couple of TEDx Talks. That's an event where people talk about a topic they think other people should know about. I had a chance to talk to a theater full of adults and some kids (including my brother) and tell them what I thought about disability and staring. I feel like the more I talk and the more information I share, the more I believe there really can be change! Kids need to know that not everyone looks the same. Not everyone acts the same. And differences can be cool. Lots of adults need to know that too. Speaking out makes it easier when a typical person meets someone with a physical disability for the first time.

MEETING NEW FRIENDS

I have a trick I use that makes it easier when I meet a new person. I'll start up a conversation with someone and get to know him or her while I hold my arms behind my back. It gives us a chance to get to know each other for a while before the new friend learns about my limb difference. I don't like when a new person's first impression of me is about my little arm. There's so much more to me than what you see on the outside. So I like to be me before the little arm can get in the way. If you know me before you're distracted, my little arm isn't as big of a deal.

I haven't had trouble making friends as I've grown up. Maybe it's because I've grown up in the same town all my life. Maybe it's because I've been so active, and I've met so many people at school, in dance classes, and on sports fields. I don't really know the secret. I do know my family doesn't hide. We do a lot!

When I'm in a big crowd, I'll sometimes use my hand to cover my little arm to avoid standing out. I'm not embarrassed by how I look; I just don't always feel like being stared at everywhere I go. Sometimes I just want a break from that. On other days, I don't care and I don't hide. It depends on my mood.

One time, my mom and I sat down at an open table at the Boston Public Market to enjoy some chowder, and a mom, daughter, and son sat across from us eating ice cream. Immediately, their eyes locked onto my little arm. Usually, we can break the stare and ask if a staring person has any questions. But the three of them never stopped staring. My mom and I were so amazed that they never looked away while eating their ice cream. I decided to hide my arm in my purse, and they STILL didn't stop! Eventually, they finished the ice cream, quietly got up, and walked away. It was so strange. Most of the time, we can turn staring into a conversation. That didn't happen at the public market! Thinking about it now, I kind of wish I had slammed my little arm on the table and yelled, "Wanna talk about it?" It would have been fun to see how they'd react! Maybe I'll do that the next time I feel like I'm in an awkward staring situation. And it just shows how important it is for me to keep doing what I'm doing—hopefully the next time they encounter someone with a physical difference, they won't be so afraid to just ask.

4
FAMILY AND FRIENDS

Some of the most important people in my life are my friends! For most of my life, I lived across the street from my two best friends in the world. They're identical twins, Quin and Reese. We've known one another since before we were born! My mom met the twins' mom at a party while they were pregnant with us. I was born a few weeks later, and my besties were born a few months after that. We went to the same school until I moved a mile away and had to change elementary schools. It was worth it for the chance to live alongside a lake. Luckily, we've found all kinds of ways to be together—different activities and as many sleepovers as possible. The girls' mom says we're actually triplets, because that's how close we are. That also means we don't always get along, but we love one another very much. Sometimes we disagree, but we always make up in the end.

I'm excited Quin and Reese are going to the same middle school as I am. Through the years, they've always had my back. I have always tried to have friends around who I can lean on to help me deal with people and tiny problems I might have. When I was younger, if I had trouble buttoning a pair of pants or zipping a jacket, I would have a friend help me out. I have made a point of doing everything by myself, but when I need someone, I'm not afraid to ask. Plus, that means I don't need to rely on teachers or other adults as much. I would rather lean on my friends than on grown-ups.

Recently, the girls had a birthday and decided that instead of having a huge party, they only wanted to celebrate it with me. Our families traveled a couple of hours away from our town to a hotel that has a water park inside.

We let our brothers stay with my parents while we stayed in a room with Quin and Reese's parents. We had an amazing time playing in the water, being goofy, and just not caring about what anyone thought of us. I think that's what makes the girls such great friends. We support one another. I feel like I can be the real me without worrying about what Quin or Reese will say.

Friends are so important, and I am lucky to have made friends all over the country, thanks to all our travel and the Born Just Right community. But the ones who are the most important to me are all the great friends I've made at school and through my activities.

FRIENDS KEEP CHANGING

As I get older, friendships can be kind of strange. When I hang out with my friends, I've noticed we all have a lot of feelings and we can easily get angry at one another. But when something really bad is happening around us, my friends will stop and back me up. It isn't often that

I have problems with other people, but there have been times when a kid gives me extra trouble.

Sometimes my friends and I have fun with my little arm. A few years ago, I remember having a regular problem during recess. There was a kid who couldn't stop being dramatic and talking about my little arm all the time. It was funny at first, but it got annoying after weeks and weeks of the same reaction. Eventually, my friends and I decided to have fun with it. Every time the kid would gasp and stare, I'd say that I didn't eat pickles, so I got a pickle-shaped arm. Yes, it's silly. But it was a fun joke to have with my friends, and it really did get the kid to leave me alone.

Most of my friends and I talk at school or on our phones, mostly through FaceTime or text message. I'm in a couple of group texts that can talk about all kinds of things . . . but I try not to type anything that can get me into trouble. At some point, group texts seem to lead to drama. But they also help us decide what to wear to school!

I also connect with my friends online. I e-mail with a few. Others I talk to on Instagram or Facebook. My mom watches what I post really closely, so I am careful to think about what I say and share. But it's really cool to be able to see people I know who live in other parts of the country or the world!

SCHOOL AND FRIENDS

Living in the same town and the same school district my whole life means I keep finding more opportunities to make more friends. But as I get older, there are also a lot more people who judge me. I don't think it's just because I have a little arm. I think it's more because I stand out. I have a lot of opinions, and I get caught talking when I should be paying attention. Any time I make a tiny mistake at school, I get called out for it. That happens with kids and teachers. It drives me crazy. A lot of times, I will be the one to get in trouble even if a group of us are doing something we shouldn't. It happens to me a lot. I get annoyed and try not to react poorly to my teachers, but my facial expressions always give me away. My mom says I need to work on my poker face. Whenever I try to do a poker face, I just end up laughing.

I've had some really great teachers, but one of my favorite teachers helped me wrap up elementary school. I was always stubborn about taking time to read books, but my fifth-grade teacher, Mrs. Wilcoxson, somehow got me reading more than I'd ever read before. She encouraged me to read just a little every single day. I'd heard teachers say that before, but this time I really took the advice seriously. These days, I can't stop reading all kinds of books, especially mysteries and historical fiction stories. Along with reading, my teacher was always willing to stick up for me when I needed a little support from a grown-up. She also wasn't afraid to call me out for making bad choices. I think that's what made her such a great teacher. Plus, she had a really good sense of humor. Everyone needs a laugh sometimes at school.

5
CAMP NO LIMITS

Have you ever traveled somewhere new but instantly felt at home? That's how I feel when I go to Camp No Limits. It's one of my favorite places to visit in the whole world.

My mom says she discovered the camp while searching the Internet when I was really little. Just like everything else, my parents wanted to make sure I had all the experiences many other kids my age had. She decided I was old enough to attend for the first time when I was three years old, and she felt like Camp No Limits would be a great fit. I have tried not to miss out on the camp ever since. Camp No Limits happens in a lot of different locations each year. I'm lucky there is one that started in my state. We can drive there!

Camp No Limits is a family camp where kids with limb differences, their siblings, and their parents can go to camp together. The first time my family attended camp, I was hooked. I was around older kids who looked like me—that had never happened before. The first couple of years, there weren't a lot of families, but the kids who were there were important to me. They're still the people I consider my first mentors. They taught me how to tie my shoes. They taught me ways to do my hair. They taught me how I have friends who really understand what it's like to be different. Camp No Limits happens here in Missouri, but it also happens in a lot of other places in the United States. I've had a chance to attend a couple of others out of state, and those feel just like home to me too. No matter where camp is, I'm with family.

The Missouri camp is on a hilly spot next to a river. We drive through twists and turns for what feels like forever to get there. When you first drive up, you see a big hotel-looking building. Then you walk down a steep hill, and there's a beach, a mini-golf course, and a bunch of smaller cabins. For some reason, the weather is usually sticky and hot. In most cases, you'd catch me enjoying the air-conditioning inside. But at camp, all I want to do is play outside. There are families and kids everywhere—and best of all, a lot of those kids look like me! Even though I participate in a ton of sports and other clubs and activities at home, camp is the only place where I know I won't be "different" to most other people.

When we first arrive, everyone from camp meets up in the meeting hall. We introduce ourselves to new people, snag camp T-shirts, and get the chance to just be silly. There's something magical that happens when a bunch of kids with limb differences meet. We have an instant connection. We may not all agree on the same things, and we may have different challenges, but we have an understanding. It feels so natural and comfortable. I don't have many places I go where I can feel like myself and relax. Camp No Limits is one of them.

At camp, I feel excited and ready to learn new skills and ways to be strong. I have extra energy in my body, and I am so comfortable around everyone—the camp counselors, and the kids and their families.

I can thank camp for introducing me to some amazing mentors, some of whom are limb-different teens and adults. It is really cool to know that I'm not alone and that I can learn from older people who have been there. I learned skills like zipping zippers, tying shoes, and buttoning buttons at camp. I even learned tips on how to put my hair into a ponytail. Those may not seem like challenging tasks, but you have to work a lot harder on learning those skills with one hand!

The person I think about the most at Camp No Limits is one of the mentors, Joshua Kennison. Josh (the name I use with him) was born without hands, feet, or a tongue! He has attended so many of the camps and is an amazing coach to kids, especially me.

The first time I met him, I was four years old. We became instant friends. From my memories back when I met him, I remember climbing up on Josh's lap and just laughing with him. Josh is so comfortable being himself. He looks different, but he is so easy to get to know. He helps me feel more comfortable with my differences. Even more amazing, Josh is one of the fastest people I've ever met. For a while, he was on the U.S. Paralympic Track and Field team as a sprinter and long jumper. When he runs, you can barely see him as he zooms by.

It isn't Josh's speed that makes him special. For me, I feel lucky to have a mentor who grew up knowing what it's like to be different and wanting to help others. Josh has talked to me a bunch of times over Skype, and I see him most summers at Camp No Limits. We've even had a chance to visit a couple of times when I travel to Maine (where he lives). He's taught me a lot, not just in ways that help me as a kid. He's also taught me how to be a mentor and help younger kids.

Because of people like Josh, I enjoy finding the younger, shy kids and talking to them. One of my best memories of camp is working with a younger camper and helping her learn how to tie her shoes. She was having a hard time.

"I can't do it," she kept saying each time her attempts weren't quite working out. She was crying, and I could tell she was really frustrated.

I looked her in the eye and said, "'Can't' isn't a word I use." I knew she could do it, even if, in the moment, it felt like she couldn't. But the next day, she did it! After just one day of getting super frustrated, she was so happy. We all cheered and were so proud. That feeling of pride is something I love thinking back on when I talk about Camp No Limits. I love teaching life skills like buttoning buttons and tying shoes. Those are skills I learned from older campers, and from my own attempts at figuring these things out! It's so cool to know I'm helping younger kids learn things I needed to know, because they need to know them too.

The limb-different kids get to learn life skills through physical and occupational therapy, but we get to do a lot of typical camp stuff too! For example, we learn about Pilates and how important it is to keep a strong core. (My stomach muscles are super strong.) The founder and executive director, Mary Leighton, tells us all how a strong core helps everyone—no matter how many limbs you do or do not have!

It's not all hard work during camp. Every year, I get to make new friends and play. My favorite part is swimming. The camp is next to a beautiful lake, kind of like the one next to our house in Columbia. It has a sandy beach where we can play for hours. When you look along the water, you'll see a pile of helper legs that kids left on the edge before they jumped in to get wet. Each year, the kids have to take swim tests so we can get access to all water areas without an adult. It's not easy. You have to tread water for what feels like forever, and then you have to swim laps. No one ever judges kids if they can or can't pass the test, but it's a huge motivation for us to keep getting better at swimming. I have a friend who is motivated to pass that test. She has seen a lot of our friends pass, and she wants to be able to join us too! She hasn't passed the test yet, but she's determined to do so, and I know it's going to happen one of these days. And we are going to help her however we can. Everyone accepts one another and all the different ways we look. It is a great feeling I carry with me all year.

My brother used to go to Camp No Limits with me when he was younger too. My mom has been able to attend almost every summer with me. My dad has to stay at work mostly, but he's been able to attend a couple of times too. Camp No Limits is an extended family for all of us.

OH, BOY! CAMP JOY!

In addition to Camp No Limits, I recently had a chance to start attending a whole new camp that's nicknamed Amp Camp. It's really called Paddy Rossbach Youth Camp, and it's run by the Amputee Coalition. That's a big national organization that supports people with amputations and people who are born with limb differences.

This camp is different because we camper kids leave our families behind. We get to fly to camp all by ourselves. The first time I went to camp, I was so nervous flying by myself, but when I got there, I met so many new and old friends, including a couple of Camp No Limits campers! Kids stay in cabins in their different age groups, and there are separate boys' and girls' cabins. Instead of life skills and family support, the camp is focused totally on kids doing kid stuff. We swim, make crafts, and even have a camp dance. I don't have to be a mentor. I don't have to teach. I just get to be a kid surrounded by other kids who have the same kind of differences. Even most of the camp counselors have limb differences! Camp No Limits has limb-different mentors, but Amp Camp seems to have even more. I have never experienced feeling as normal as I do at that camp.

I am lucky to attend both camps each year. It feels really good to be able to get away and just be me, without any judgment. The kids I hang out with at both camps deal with the same stuff I manage in real non-camp life. We just understand.

MEETING KIDS WITH DIFFERENCES EVERYWHERE

Beyond camps, I have traveled a lot as a kid. My parents take Cameron and me to Maine every year. Sometimes we stop off along our drive up and hang out with other Born Just Right families in the Northeast. These are families we've met through my mom's writing online. It's always nice to know that there is a friendly face who can totally understand the experiences you are going through. Like at the camps, we don't have to take on the added responsibility of having to explain everything— we just know and can compare any challenges we might be having, or just enjoy hanging out.

When we drive home from Maine, we always stay with a limb-difference family that we've known for what feels like forever. Driving between Missouri and Maine is a two-day trip, so when we get to our friends' place, we're usually tired. They always give us great food, and it's nice to hang out with friends. We don't sleep a lot because we play games and laugh. We rarely miss our chance to see one another, and it's a really great way to end a vacation.

We also have met with kids and families through organizations like Helping Hands Foundation and Sammy's Friends. Helping Hands is an organization in Massachusetts that has a family event in the summer and in the winter. We've had a chance to attend those events a few times through the years. Sammy's Friends is the first online group my mom found when I was born. It's still a small group of families, and we try to see them whenever we can. Each and every time I get to meet more kids like me, the less I feel alone. The older I get, the more I realize my experiences really can help a lot of younger kids as they grow up. If my mom hadn't written so much about me, I don't know if we'd know so many people. I am also happy I can meet with kids everywhere I go to share my tips and advice while learning from other limb-different kids at the same time.

Besides my amazing counselor Josh, another limb-different adult and mentor who has really given me support is a guy named Ryan Haack. He has a website called Living One-Handed, and he even wrote a super-sweet book called *Different Is Awesome*. Ryan is a great friend to my whole family, and he's always had such a positive attitude about his one-handed life. We met him through the Sammy's Friends group. My mom connected with him, and we've tried to see each other at events like Helping Hands and Born Just Right meetups.

Meeting other people who have physical differences has helped me realize that what you and I think is "normal" can be totally different! To you, a one-handed person may sound strange. But to me, having two hands seems totally unusual! Maybe using a wheelchair is different to you. To a kid using a wheelchair, it's a super-helpful tool that helps him or her have the freedom to move! It's just how we think about it.

Summer camps with limb-different kids inspire me to be okay with the way I see things. They motivate me to raise money so other families can have the kind of experiences I've had throughout most of my life. When it comes to Camp No Limits, I am able to attend every year because of a local fund that pays for my fees. Since my camp is paid for, each year I ask friends and family to donate to camp instead of giving me gifts. We've sent dozens of kids to Camp No Limits! It feels really good knowing I can bring happy experiences to others.

6
LIMITLESS

My time at Camp No Limits taught me a really important thing about fitness, and it's stuck with me as I've grown up. As I mentioned earlier, it's very important for me to have strong core muscles. If my neck and torso are super strong, I'm less likely to have problems with my shoulders, arms, and legs. That's why I look at sports and being as active as possible as a way to stay strong. My mom started focusing on those lessons pretty early on.

DANCE CLASS BALANCE

My mom got me started with dance class when I was a toddler. I didn't start walking until I was eighteen months old, so dancing was a chance to help me improve my balance and learn to do things like skip! I thought it was fun to put on the costumes and dance around with my friends. I didn't know it was helping me get strong back then.

Dance classes start with the basics, and my studio required tap and ballet before I could take anything advanced. I took classes every year until I got good enough to take hip-hop and musical theater classes. I loved all of it. I practiced once or twice a week, and then there was a big performance—a recital or showcase—at the end of the year. It was awesome to show all my friends and family what I'd been doing! Plus, the hair, the makeup, the fancy costumes—it was all so fun. It was an extra bonus to working so hard all year.

Most of my dance teachers were really good about making sure other kids and parents knew my limb difference wasn't going to prevent me from doing anything in class. I sometimes tried dances with my helper arms, but they always seemed to be more awkward than helpful. My helper arms feel too big and bulky to help with dancing. One year, we had a costume that included gloves. My mom just turned the left glove into an arm sleeve so I matched everyone else.

I stopped dance when I started adding on a lot of sports and Girl Scout activities. My parents said they couldn't drive me to any more activities, so I had to pick at least one to end. I am kind of sad I stopped the dance classes, but I still take what I've learned from them and apply it to my other activities—and it gave me a lot of confidence! I still like to dance a lot, just not in formal classes anymore.

SPORTS

I really love all my different sports teams. I'm very competitive. I often feel like I'm competing to prove I can be an athlete to others, and then there are times when I compete with myself to see how far I can push my limits. I've leaned on sports as a way to help me feel strong and to show how I am able to do anything.

When I started out in dance, my parents also put me on a soccer team. While I clearly loved dance, I actually hated soccer when I first started. (For some reason, the one sport that doesn't need hands is the one sport I'm least interested in playing!) Once they realized how much I disliked it, they had me try others to see what might stick. Since then, I've tried so many different sports. I enjoy ones that involve hands, like basketball and softball. Maybe it's because I like the challenge. Maybe it's just because these sports don't bore me. Whatever it is, I've figured out all kinds of different ways to play!

My favorite sport to play these days is basketball. I started playing through a club in our town when I was in third grade. I like running and shooting the ball, but my favorite part is playing defense. My little arm is an awesome jabbing weapon to steal the ball from the other team. Most of the time I don't get called for a foul when

I jab a little here and there. Basketball is a fast game, and it never gets boring . . . unless I'm on the bench waiting to get back on the floor. I can't stand sitting on the bench.

Being part of a team is a lot of fun. Since I wanted to get better at basketball, I started going to a sports camp that focuses on helping kids with limb differences play really well. It's called NubAbility Athletics. This is a camp that is totally different from Camp No Limits. It's a huge camp that focuses on teaching kids how to play elite-level sports, even if they have different limbs. I have gotten tips on basketball, softball, track and field, and all kinds of other sports from some amazing athletes. Many of them have played sports at the college level or even in the Paralympics. While I had a chance to get better at my basketball and softball skills at NubAbility, I also discovered another way to exercise: CrossFit.

CrossFit is a fitness program that really challenges your body. It uses a variety of high-intensity moves and weight-bearing exercises that you do in different combinations. I have become really strong after doing this for three years. I can jump up on boxes, lift weights, and do all kinds of other exercises. I work out with some older girls who make me want to get better. My coaches have found ways to change some of the exercise challenges so I can do similar workouts, even if they usually need two hands. Changing the workout to fit my body is called Adaptive CrossFit. It's a lot of fun, and I'm usually really sore afterward.

One of my favorite workouts is possible because of a one-handed adaptive jump rope. It's a stick with a rope attached on each side. I rotate it with one hand while I jump. It took me a while to figure out how to make it work, but I can do it! I also figured out a really fun way to do push-ups by rolling my little arm on a medicine ball while I push up with my full arm. I also know how to do push-ups with one arm. My parents aren't big fans of any exercise that has me using only one side of my body. That's why I'm always looking for new ways to adapt a workout. There are a ton of adaptive athletes on Instagram. We often look there to get fresh ideas and talk to the athletes for tips.

People are always asking me how I do what I do in sports. I did not grow up thinking sports were impossible. Thanks to my family, and the combination of Camp No Limits, Amp Camp, and NubAbility, I have been taught that everything is possible; I just might have to do it differently. When people look at me, they might think of a lot of *can't*s, but I honestly don't instantly think I can't when I have a challenge. I want to try it all, and so far, I've had a chance to do a lot.

OTHER ACTIVITIES

I don't just participate in sports; I've also taken piano lessons since I was in second grade. My family loves live music, so taking lessons and learning to enjoy it is a natural part of our lives. My brother started playing piano in second grade, so my mom had me start at the same age. The very first day I started, my piano teacher expected to teach me one-handed music. But that was never something I considered. I told her I wanted to play with my hand and my little arm. Since then, she's found music that fits my abilities. Sometimes she even rewrites the songs for me.

In the last couple of years, my piano teacher has also started giving me voice lessons. I love to sing, and I hope working with her will help me get even better. To be honest, I think I like singing more than playing piano. But my piano teacher says I should keep playing piano until my voice matures so I really understand music theory before I focus on singing.

I was lucky to sing in my school choir, and I was even invited to my school district honors choir. The biggest opportunity I've had in choir was getting the chance to sing a solo in my final elementary school choir concert. I had a plan the moment my choir director presented the song to us—I would practice and practice and do the best possible audition. I don't know how many times I rehearsed before that day, but I gave it my all. During my singing audition, my choir director was impressed I had already memorized the song. Even better, she gave me the solo!

I got to perform the solo in front of the school, and a couple of times in front of a large audience. It was so cool to watch people react to my singing. I'm not bad, and because I practiced so much, I know I gave my best performances.

Music is an outlet to just let things go. I love singing in choirs because it's a totally different kind of team. Voices together make such an amazing sound. When I perform with a group, I don't really notice the audience . . . even if I get a little nervous before a show. I hope I can use the work I've done so far to help me get involved in middle school shows! I have plans to try out for all the dramas and musicals I can.

PERSPECTIVE-CHANGING TRAVEL

I think travel is another reason I sometimes feel limitless. Because I live in Missouri, I know some people who have never seen the ocean. I'm very lucky to have never had that problem. My family drives to Maine every year, and my parents have made that trip since even before Cameron and I were born! It's a chance to spend time with my grandparents who have a house on the ocean. The Maine house is perfect. We get to stare at the ocean from the porch, eat yummy food, and play in the water every day. I learned to kayak there, and it's the first place I learned to ride a bike without training wheels.

The car rides to Maine are long. Really long. But Cameron and I sit in the back seat reading books, watching every single movie we can, and eventually finding reasons to fight. My mom supplies the snacks and usually tries to stop the battles. My dad does a lot of the driving, with my mom as a backup. He often says how he'd rather drive than try to stop Cameron and me from fighting. We bring our dogs along for the ride, which makes me really happy. Our dog Bailey thinks motorcycles are dangerous and barks at them. That makes me laugh every time! We spend almost twenty-four hours in the car, but the drive is worth it.

The Maine house sits on the edge of a hill that looks out at an ocean cove. There's a wraparound porch, where you can sit on rocking chairs and just stare at everything beautiful. You can hear the waves crashing into rocks and watch seagulls fly around. Sometimes there are sailboats that float by. And there are always lobster boats out with lobstermen and lobsterwomen working to catch someone's dinner! If you think it's peaceful to sit near the lake by my house, try sitting by the rocky ocean in Maine. Listening to the tide move up and down our cove can put me into a trance. I love having the chance to soak in nature!

My parents got us an ocean kayak that lets us paddle out into our cove and out into the rolling waves of the ocean. It's amazing to float in the water and feel so tiny, with water and rocks and the huge blue sky. The ocean is so quiet when I'm floating out there. All my problems in the world disappear . . . at least until my brother splashes me with his paddle! And yes, if you're wondering, I can paddle a kayak. I have a helper arm that I can paddle with. But I can also paddle without a helper arm!

Every year, my mom makes sure she gets a picture of Cameron and me on the same spot on the rocks near the

Maine house. There's a picture of me on that spot from every year we've visited since I was six months old. It's a little piece of tradition that makes me roll my eyes, but it is really cool when you can see all the years of photos. My brother and I were SO TINY! It also gives me a chance to look back and realize how lucky we are to escape and relax each year.

Our Maine trip is full of traditions. We always have rock-skipping contests and ice-cream-eating contests. My grandpa and I even have a scrambled-egg-cooking contest. We have lobster races and go on hikes and play at nearby beaches. We eat at some of the same restaurants every year because they're so yummy. Maine is kind of a home away from home. I sometimes forget that not everyone gets to go to a special spot like ours.

We also drive down to South Florida to visit my grandparents' house every other year. We celebrate Christmas, and because we have to drive home, we stop in Orlando to visit Walt Disney World. I'm a December baby, so I get to celebrate my birthday at Walt Disney World! I am SO lucky. I have celebrated half of my birthdays at my happy place. My parents, Cameron, and I are really good at having fun in the parks. I always feel free to be me even though there are so many people at Disney World. Yes, some people stare at me, but I'm too busy having fun to really worry about it.

When I was three, during a birthday trip, my mom surprised me with a really puffy dress and a chance to get my hair done at a fancy Disney boutique called Bibbidi Bobbidi Boutique. I was turned into a princess, and I got to walk around the Magic Kingdom looking beautiful. I loved it so much, I have dressed up for a lot of my Disney birthdays. I love to dress up. My dad says I was so dressed up, people were staring and pointing at me, not because of my little arm but because I was so fancy! I kind of think I'm getting too old for that kind of fun . . . but I don't think I'm ready to put away all the fancy outfits. I don't usually dress up like that anywhere else other than Disney World. I'm both a tomboy and a dressy person. Most of the time, you'll catch me wearing a shirt and leggings or a T-shirt and shorts. But I think my Disney World trips helped grow my love of sparkles.

At Disney World, glitter is called pixie dust! I know those trips added to my love of shiny things.

One really amazing visit to Disney World happened after my mom and I attended an Amputee Coalition national conference. I had never attended a conference before, but I loved hearing experts talk about the new ways they're building helper arms for adults. (There isn't a lot of research done about kids and prosthetics yet.) My mom introduced me to one of the men who helped invent a prosthetic tail for a dolphin that lives in Florida. The dolphin's name is Winter, and she's alive thanks to the invention of that helper tail. The man invited my family and me to meet Winter the dolphin in person *and* sent us to Walt Disney World! Can you believe that?

The trip to Disney was awesome, but the time I spent with Winter changed my view on prosthetics. I learned that Winter doesn't wear her helper tail all the time, which made me feel better. Imagine connecting a hunk of plastic onto your body all the time. I know exactly what that is like, and it feels like a burden sometimes.

I know Winter the dolphin feels the same way about prosthetics. When I had the chance to meet her, I learned she wears her helper tail for about an hour a day while she works with a therapist. I'm not the only one who has to work with therapists! That one-hour therapy session is long enough to keep her body from breaking. When she doesn't wear a tail, she swims side to side like a fish. With her helper tail, she swims up and down. That fish-swimming style is really bad on her spine, so her helper tail keeps her from getting really hurt. That's also why my parents want me to wear my helper arms. I need to wear prosthetics to keep my body from getting hurt when I'm older. When I met Winter, it finally made sense. I stopped fighting it as much. I started seeing why prosthetics can be helpful. Also, I got super wet when Winter splashed my brother and me during our meeting!

Not only have I gotten the chance to meet a limb-different dolphin, but I've also had a chance to travel and hang out with a lot of kids with differences thanks to Born Just Right, Camp No Limits, and Amp Camp.

Most of the kids I have met have a limb difference from being born that way, having an accident, or getting sick. But getting the chance to attend the Wounded Warrior Amputee Softball Team (WWAST) Kids Camp let me meet members of the military who are amputees. ("Amputee" is another word for someone who lost a leg or an arm.) The members of WWAST lost limbs from bombings or attacks during war or from accidents. Every player has lost at least one limb, but they play softball really well! The team travels across the country playing against fully-limbed softball teams. They show all kinds of communities how a physical difference doesn't have to hold you back.

Each year, a small group of kids get a once-in-a-lifetime chance to spend a week with the team to learn how to improve their softball skills. But it's so much more than that. It wasn't really a camp. The whole week was an *experience*. I also got to see and do some really fun things in Southern California. We saw dolphins, explored parks and beaches, and even spent a VIP day at Disneyland! But the biggest, most fun part was on the last day of the camp when we all got to participate in a big softball game with a huge crowd at a baseball stadium. Hearing my name called out as I walked up to the plate and making a base hit was unreal. There were people with signs in the stands cheering for me! I made friends during the kids' camp who I'll never forget. I also have new mentors I can look up to. Even better, the WWAST started inviting kids back for a reunion each year. The kids meet each year in Branson, which is another spot in Missouri that is only a three-hour drive from us!

Each and every trip I take is a new experience that helps me see the world as a bigger place. I get to meet so many cool people along the way.

7
INTRODUCTION TO DESIGN/PROJECT UNICORN

I guess you could say I have been designing all my life. Working with Mr. David really sparked my interest in design and how things are built and how they work. But what I didn't realize was that all those experiences with prosthetics set me up to learn how my thoughts on design could lead toward some really nontraditional ideas. One of my travel opportunities gave me a chance to spend a week in San Francisco for a camp called Superhero Cyborgs. I was invited to join four other kids with limb differences to learn about design. I didn't even realize I loved design before I had this experience! The camp's codirector, Kate Ganim, issued a challenge that took my life in directions I never could have imagined. We were asked a simple question: If you could build something for your little arm that helped you become a superhero, what kind of superhero would you be?

ARE YOU A DESIGNER?

You might be surprised to find out you're a designer in the making. If you have done any of these things, you might want to give designing a try:

- Created slime

- Built with Legos

- Designed and created jewelry

- Designed your own buildings and structures in Minecraft

- Played with bubbles or balloons

- Drawn pictures

- Played with clay

- Created an outfit in an unusual or
  different way

- Taken a regular household item and turned
  it into a toy or something different

- Cooked a meal with or without directions
  (or a little bit of both)

- Creativity in ANY form can lead to design!

Our first day was focused on learning about one another and understanding how to brainstorm. My friend Sydney and I decided we really wanted to be able to shoot something out of our little arms. Syd chose water, and I chose glitter.

The camp gave us a chance to think up our designs without our parents in the room. I'm pretty sure that's why I was able to get away with the glitter idea. My mom was never very crafty, so she didn't really let me buy messy stuff before going to this camp. Once she found out I was going to work with sparkles, she couldn't really do anything other than roll her eyes (with a smile on her face).

Superhero Cyborgs happened at an amazing building along the San Francisco water. Autodesk, a company known for 3-D design software, hosted us. We got to see all the different 3-D design work they do and even got to visit a supersecret robot area! Autodesk is printing things as big as bridges and as small as skin cells! I'd never had a chance to see so many different types of ideas in one place. People can actually do this as a career! It totally shifted what I thought I wanted to do when I grow up.

Each morning, we would send the parents away and build our concepts or prototypes. We took casts of our arms, like I do with Mr. David, but we also used 3-D scanners to build our designs around the shapes of our arms on a computer. The camp counselors taught us how to use a 3-D design program and build our own ideas. I had never done anything like it before. After our camp activities, we would go on small adventures around San Francisco. We had to climb this huge hill to get there each day. It was exhausting, but we were able to see so much of the city. San Francisco is so different from where I live! I decided before we left that San Francisco is one of my favorite places. This wasn't the first time I had a chance to visit the city, but it was the first time I really felt like I was living there instead of just being a tourist.

★　★　★

Besides the awesome experience of hanging out in San Francisco, it was so fun to see my designs come to life in a totally new way, different from what I had ever experienced before. If you've written something on a computer and printed it out, there's something really cool about seeing your work on paper. Think of how amazing it can be when you design a thing on a computer, and then you can watch a 3-D printer actually create that thing in real life. Instead of ink, 3-D printers use really thin layers of melted plastic to build exactly what you created on your computer.

As I worked on my idea to shoot glitter from my arm, I learned one of the most important lessons of being a designer: *failure.* I really hate messing things up. (I got that from my mom.) But when you are designing an idea, you have to mess up. You can't design an idea without failure.

I finally came up with my first big solution: a starburst design that wrapped around my arm. I used five plastic air bulbs and put plastic glove fingertips on top of each bulb. I poked a hole in each glove tip so air could puff out. Then I attached Nerf gun bullets on top of each bulb. I cut off the top of each bullet and filled it up with glitter. Finally, I attached a string around all the air bulbs, put the starburst around my arm, pulled the string, and . . .

Glitter just kind of spilled out. It was a cool glitter cannon, but not cool enough. I knew I wanted to keep working!

★   ★   ★

On the last day of our camp, we all got to show off our inventions to people who work at Autodesk. It was so much fun, and I ended up spreading glitter on one of the camp counselors who helped me learn how to use a 3-D printer. It was so funny! I also got to introduce my invention with an official name: Project Unicorn. I came up with the name when I was thinking about my work with glitter. To me, unicorns are happy and sparkly. So why not include unicorns in my project? With that name and after discovering how much fun it is to shoot glitter, there was no turning back!

PROJECT UNICORN

The Superhero Cyborgs camp wasn't totally over after I got home. I was assigned a design partner who I was supposed to work with to keep making my design better. All the kids involved in the camp were given different design partners and three months to try to come up with bigger and better ideas for our superhero projects.

I was partnered with a designer named Sam Hobish. Sam is an industrial designer with a side of graphic design. He volunteered to work with me while he was working at Autodesk. He's moved away from San Francisco, but we're still working together. He's like a brother who is older than my brother. He also makes me laugh.

Sam and I met over Google Hangouts every Friday after school. We brainstormed and worked over our computers to come up with new ideas. Sometimes Sam would print stuff out and send it to me in the mail, and I'd work on trying to improve the idea. I hit some big walls when we realized we couldn't build my idea out with any kind of traditional-looking 3-D printed helper arms. We needed to do something different. I didn't need a replacement hand—I needed a glitter blaster!

I posted some of my experiences from camp and the building process on YouTube. My mom was taking pictures of my meetings with Sam and sharing them to her blog and to social media sites. He and I were just brainstorming about ways to work with my idea. For a while, we thought we were going to build an arm that *looked* like an arm. But after a few concepts didn't work out, we stepped away and thought outside the box of what my arm could look like. It's kind of amazing how well we worked together since we'd never met in person. Video chats are cool like that.

Sam and I were working hard and taking all kinds of notes, photos, and videos. At some point, a journalist asked to interview me about my work, and it ended up becoming an article on a website. Suddenly, during my spring break from school, a YouTube video of me showing off my glitter cannon was all over the place. I was interviewed by all kinds of news websites and television stations. I was so excited when there were articles about my invention on the Nerdist website and on Amy Poehler's Smart Girls. Kid President actually tweeted about me. When I saw that, I ran around the house in circles screaming with excitement!

Getting the chance to see my idea online and receiving attention was a lot of fun. It was a chance for me to talk about limb differences in a fun way. Two-handed kids can't shoot glitter like I can! I created something fun that limb-different kids can enjoy. All the two-handed kids and adults I talked to wanted to learn more and see how it worked! I had young kids tell me they were jealous of my little arm. How amazing is that?

SHARING FAR AND WIDE

That little burst of attention was just the beginning for me and Project Unicorn. Sam and I were still working on new ideas when we found out all the Superhero Cyborgs kids had a chance to present our work at

Maker Faire Bay Area. That's one of the biggest events in the country that lets adults and kids show off the stuff they've created. Knowing we were presenting to Maker Faire, Sam and I worked really hard on coming up with a new design that could shoot glitter faster than my old glitter cannon. Plus, I had a chance to go back to San Francisco!

When I met up with Sam in San Francisco a day before Maker Faire, it was the first time we had ever met in person. It felt like we'd always known each other. The way we talked over Google Hangouts was totally the same way we talked to each other in person. We are really silly together. I guess that's what you would expect if you're working on a project that shoots glitter!

Instead of a starburst design, Sam and I came up with a long unicorn horn that fit on my arm. Glitter can shoot right out of the end of the horn. The invention didn't look like a hand at all, and that's just the way I liked it. We used little tubes of glitter that were like bullets. To get the glitter to spray out, a plastic tube is attached to the horn and connected to a compressed-air can. Compressed air is the stuff you find at an office-supply store that is used to help clean computer keyboards. It has a strong spray of air, but it isn't strong enough to hurt someone if they get hit with glitter in the face! Compressed air is SO much better than just pulling a string and trying to get the air to puff out the glitter. Sam came up with an idea where I'd have extra glitter bullets on a sleeve that I wore on my arm and another collection of them on my leg. That gave me the chance to reload glitter as quickly as possible. It also made me look extra tough! I was a real superhero.

The hardest part was getting the glitter into the little tubes. My mom was in charge of that part. I think that's really funny, since she didn't like glitter and suddenly she was in charge of loading it into small containers. She ended up spilling it all over the place. I think this was the beginning of a new life for us. There always seems to be a little bit of glitter on our clothes. I'm not complaining! It's just a part of our world now.

Each of my other Superhero Cyborgs camp friends and I got to give five-minute talks on a main Maker

Faire stage where people showed off their work all day. Everywhere you walk at the Faire, you see people showing off cool ideas. It really is like show-and-tell at school. The Maker Faire show-and-tell version is way bigger and includes so many adults. There were people walking around dressed up as robots and dinosaurs. There were displays and crafts. I wish I could have spent even more time there!

One of the things Sam and I figured out while we practiced for the Maker Faire demonstration was that the size of the glitter matters. When the glitter is smaller, it doesn't stick as much to the glitter cannon. The smaller glitter also seems to be able to wash off of hands and clothes easier. Sam bought a bunch of different types of glitter, and all of it was too chunky. It didn't spray well. My mom had to go on a hunt around San Francisco for new glitter. Somehow, there was a type of glitter she found at Walgreens that worked perfectly.

During the Maker Faire presentation, I got to spray the glitter on one of the people who works at Autodesk right after my friend Sydney had sprayed him with water.

The glitter really stuck on him, and it was *so* funny. I had kids running up to me afterward asking if I could spray them with glitter. Everyone I talked to about Project Unicorn laughed and smiled. I realized, *You can never be sad with sparkles.* So many people were paying attention to my work because this idea was a lot of fun, and it happened to work really well for a little arm! Something that makes me different made it possible for me to be an inventor who sees things differently. I also think all the years I have spent working on helper arms with Mr. David helped a lot. I was a part of the maker world before realizing it!

After Maker Faire, I was invited to attend a maker health event in Washington, DC, through the U.S. Department of Health and Human Services. I got to meet all kinds of adults who have invented new ways to help people with disabilities, and others who have great ideas that help people who are sick. Project Unicorn was the only project presented by a kid. I got to speak to all kinds of leaders and spread my fun and glitter. A very important person allowed me to spray him, even though he was wearing a really nice suit!

While I was in DC, I also attended the National Maker Faire. It was another big show-and-tell for all ages. It wasn't quite as big as the one in California, but I got to meet so many people and learn so much. It was also the first time someone recognized me from my work! A woman who was presenting at a table asked to take pictures with me. That was so strange and cool at the same time. I walked around with Project Unicorn, showing it off to anyone who was curious. I ended up winning an Editor's Choice Award for my idea!

Every step along the way, my mom was sharing stories on the Born Just Right website. She also shared photos and videos on social media. I think all that sharing helped me get even more opportunities to talk about Project Unicorn and tell people why I love design.

While Sam and I continued to meet over Google Hangouts and work on making Project Unicorn even better, I kept getting invited to speak and share the project. I've visited community groups in my town where I presented to adults. I've also talked to different groups of kids, like local Boy Scout troops, and even to an entire school during an assembly in St. Louis! It is so cool to share what it is like to have a limb difference and all the fun ways I can use design to take advantage of my little arm. I always tell kids and adults that design is something anyone can learn. We all have good ideas hiding in our heads. You just have to stop and think and create. I had no idea 3-D printing lets you be so creative until I got to learn how it works. Now when I have an idea, I can jump into Tinkercad (my favorite 3-D design tool) and try to make my idea real. Not every idea works, but I love being able to see my ideas come to life on a 3-D printer.

Because I keep working with Sam on projects, Autodesk and Dremel—which is a power tool and 3-D printer company—teamed up to donate a 3-D printer so that I could have my own. That means I don't have to wait for Sam to print out the ideas he and I work on. We can just share computer files! I even got a donation from another organization called the Awesome Foundation that helped pay for all the special plastic, called filament, that I use to print things.

Even though I use the printer and software for new prosthetic designs, I also like to play around with other designs to see if they will work. For example, I created a fun cell phone holder that looks like a donut. I even created custom hearts with the first initial of each kid in my class for Valentine's Day.

BIG OPPORTUNITIES

All these creations, speaking opportunities, and inventions gave me a chance to visit Walt Disney World again! This time, I visited the park to receive a special award given by the Walt Disney Company. Two other girls and I won Dream Big, Princess awards. Disney gave me the Dream Big, Princess Innovator Award for the ways I'd worked to help more people understand limb differences and create cool things. We went up on a big stage in front of a huge room of writers to accept our awards.

I got to meet some really nice people during that special Disney trip, and I made new friends. It's amazing getting to know other kids who are doing big things.

Meeting the other award winners showed me how any kid can take experiences that matter to them and make those experiences into something big.

I am shocked that I have had the chance to visit so many cool places and talk to so many people about an idea that started with glitter. I mean, look at this book! Can you believe it? I have said it time and time again— if you try really hard, you can make a change. I feel like I prove that every day. By speaking up, I can change how you think about limb differences and maybe other disabilities. Everything is possible if you believe in yourself and have support from friends and family.

THE RACHAEL RAY EXPERIENCE

If you think a trip to Walt Disney World was the ultimate experience for Project Unicorn, you would be surprised to hear I had another really amazing opportunity. It gave me a chance to make a secret trip to New York City!

I was invited to take a version of Project Unicorn to the *Rachael Ray Show*. Rachael Ray is a chef who has her own show that airs across the country. That alone sounds crazy and cool, but the visit came with a twist: I got to present my invention to the entire team from the show *Shark Tank*. The people on that show watch presentations and then decide if they want to give their own money to help businesses grow. The "sharks" ask tough questions and decide if a business can get loans. I was given the chance to share Project Unicorn with the sharks by giving a one-minute speech on the *Rachael Ray Show*. Two other kid inventions were also part of the show.

I only had a weekend to research and prepare my speech. We weren't allowed to say anything about the trip to our friends or online until the day before it went on TV. I practiced as much as I could, but I started to get really nervous. I had never talked to so many people who make big decisions with money! I really didn't want to mess up.

My mom and I flew into the city the night before the taping of the show. Even though I'd been to New York City in the past, my mom wanted to be sure I had a little fun before the big day. We walked into Times

Square and acted silly while shopping and eating good food. It was way past my bedtime by the time we got back to our hotel, but my mom kind of helped me get some of my nervousness out of my system.

The day of the show, the other kids and I had a chance to rehearse on the set of the *Rachael Ray Show*. We didn't get to actually meet the sharks or Rachael until the recording of the show. I got to go to a makeup room and get my hair done. I love adding extra curls in my super-straight, long hair. (My mom tries to add curls in my hair, but she never does it very well.) It was a lot of fun to get pampered, and it helped take some of the butterflies out of my stomach leading up to the show.

I don't think I've ever been as nervous as I was just before I walked onto the set. I was the first kid to present, and I couldn't stop worrying about what would happen if I messed up! The stage manager helped me feel less nervous by jumping up and down with me right before I walked onto the set. Thank goodness, it went really well. I had fun! I showed off Project Unicorn and a second invention that I've worked on. The sharks said they were impressed, and they even told me to keep working on my inventions. They thought I could actually sell Project Unicorn in stores! When I was done with my presentation, I went backstage, and my mom was there to hug me. I was shaking! I have never felt so proud and exhausted at the same time.

After all the kids presented their inventions, we found out we all won money to help fund our inventions that we'd just pitched! When the segment was done, we got to take a few pictures with the sharks and Rachael. It was super fast. Everything wrapped up, and before I knew it, my mom and I were in a car going back to the airport!

I went back to school and didn't talk about the experience. That felt a little strange. Luckily, it was shown on TV just a couple of days later. When TV commercials started talking about kid inventors, my life got crazy in a whole new way. Reporters at newspapers and TV news stations interviewed me. A big clip of my part of the show was shown on Facebook. It felt like a big tornado of excitement had taken over my life.

The day the kid inventor segment was shown on TV, I had to go to school! I didn't get to see it until I got home. Suddenly, my mom was juggling a new collection of interview requests. It seemed like I had a different interview every day after school. I didn't really talk about it very much at school because I didn't want to make it into a big deal. I figured if I didn't talk about it, the kids at school couldn't make fun of me or think I might have a big ego about it all. I am really proud of my work, but I don't want people to judge me more than they already do because of my arm.

The whole experience was really fun. I'm so glad I had a chance to go on a national TV show to present my idea and raise more awareness of limb differences. It feels like our life has not calmed down since. I'm excited I got to be on TV to show kids and adults that you can just be you. I didn't hide my difference—I showed it off! Even better, my limb difference wasn't a big deal. I had a chance to just be me and show off something cool without even needing to explain my physical difference.

The prize money I won on the *Rachael Ray Show* made it possible for me to buy my very own computer that is powerful enough to help me work on designs. That's a big deal because when my mom isn't in town because of work trips, I don't have a computer that works with the software I like to use. Now I can design whenever I have time. Just like sports and music practice, I know I can't get better at design without working on it as often as I can. With all my activities, that can be tricky. But luckily, my meetings continue with Sam. I also find some quiet time every once in a while to work on new ideas.

During the show, I also showed off a T-shirt that had the Project Unicorn logo that Sam and I created on the front. One of the local T-shirt makers in my town came up with the idea to put the logo in glitter on a shirt. We started selling the shirt on our website! We also started selling some of the other shirts that I've used through the years that help me feel strong. It's another way for me to design, just in a bit of a different way.

8
THE DESIGN PROCESS

For me, learning design is not hard, but it does require time. I was so lucky to attend the Superhero Cyborgs event, where I had five straight days to just brainstorm and build. It was the first time I really got to sit down and think about building something based on my own body, experiences, and interests. Have you ever had a chance to do that? I know each of the experiences I've had in my life so far has set me up to create amazing things. I just never had a chance to tap into my brain that way before. You can do it too.

Let me show you how Project Unicorn started out as a fake hand with a glove full of glitter and slowly turned into a really cool-looking unicorn horn that shoots glitter.

First, I needed to come up with an idea. I had a chance to bounce ideas off adults and kids who weren't part of my family. That created a judgment-free space to just throw fun ideas out there. I don't think you have to design away from your family, but changing your environment sometimes can help you get extra creative—and people won't just say they like it because they are your parents or your sibling!

Before we got too deep into our ideas, we got to test out how computer-aided design (CAD) works. I created a house with a chicken head on top. Why? Because I could! That's the fun thing about design. If you can make it, you can test it out and see what happens.

We also talked about the goals we wanted to reach before we walked away from our experience. I wanted to build something awesome and have fun. One kid said he wanted to create a hand with blades like the comic book character Wolverine. (Whoa!) Another kid wanted to get better at using 3-D printers.

Next, we started talking through our ideas as a group. When my friend Sydney discussed wanting to shoot water out of her little arm, I knew I also wanted to shoot something. Glitter just seemed to be the right thing for me. We each were asked to sketch out our ideas.

I envisioned a 3-D printed hand that shot sparkles. (I also didn't really know how to spell "sparkles" at the time.) With my concept, I put together a prototype. It included a hand and an arm that I cut out. I filled a plastic glove with glitter, put it over the hand, and tried to figure out how I could shoot the glitter from the fingers. It looked pretty funny. But this was when I decided to call my idea Project Unicorn. It didn't even look like a unicorn yet, but it made me happy, like a unicorn!

This was when I had a big realization. I knew using a 3-D printed hand design wasn't going to work. It hit me that I didn't need an actual hand to shoot glitter! So instead I decided to build something around my arm using CAD. I had scanned a plaster version of my arm, and I was able to build a cuff that fit. Here's what my design concept looked like at first. I thought I might want to shoot glitter from both arms.

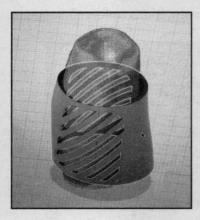

To start, I attached air puffers combined with Nerf bullets directly to a 3-D printed cuff. It wasn't very stable, but it kind of worked.

I brainstormed a few extra ideas and came up with a starburst design that could hold the puffers in place.

I took the concept I had with the air puffers, strings, and Nerf bullets and added it to the starburst. I threaded the string through the starburst to keep them in place. The final result created a glitter poof when I pulled the strings. It was cool, but I knew if I had more time, I'd create something even more powerful.

I had a lot of fun with that version, but I was motivated to keep working on ideas. That's when I teamed up with my design partner, Sam Hobish. We got to know each other, and Sam challenged me to come up with all kinds of different ideas we could possibly add to Project Unicorn. While I created different design ideas, Sam was testing different ways to force the glitter to spray. He tried CO_2 cartridges, but he realized they shot too strong and might hurt someone. That's when we worked on the idea of using compressed air.

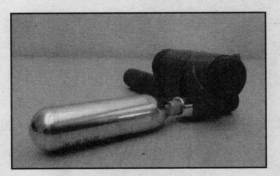

At first, we tried to go back to my idea of using a 3-D printed hand and combine a way to spray glitter out. I got so aggravated trying to get a 3-D printed hand to work, but we needed that failure to keep thinking of better and more fun ideas.

We returned to creating a tool that could spray and didn't look like what people think I need. We had a chance to come up with a really fun idea—and we did! When Sam and I met in person for the first time, Project Unicorn turned into a unicorn horn! It would shoot tiny plastic vials of glitter with the help of tubing and compressed air. We showed this version off at Maker Faires and other big events.

The cool thing was that our designs weren't done. Sam and I continued to meet online and talk about what worked and what didn't work. That's when we came up with a totally new way to shoot the tubes of glitter.

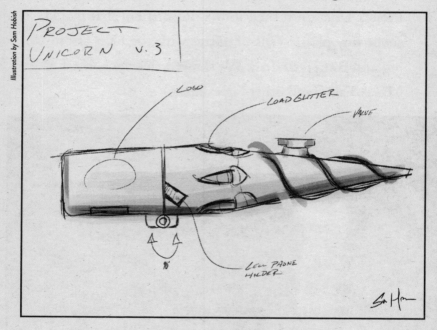

Illustration by Sam Hobish

I let Sam know that the idea of loading the glitter one tiny plastic container at a time was really annoying. I usually asked my mom to fill up the containers. It took a long time to set up, and she was super annoyed. So the concept turned into a new idea where I could fill a huge container with glitter. It still connects to an air tube and compressed air, but it's so much more fun.

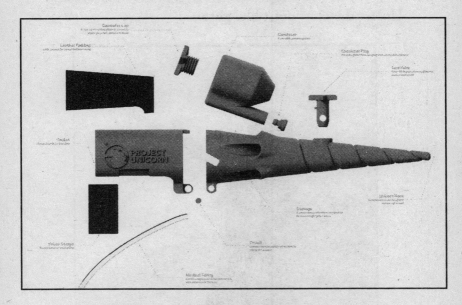

I am so proud of this version. The 3-D printed unicorn horn looks supercool. I love being able to shoot a lot of glitter all at once. But there was one more problem: we were using glitter that wasn't good for the environment. The longer I talked about Project Unicorn, the more my mom and I heard about how glitter is a micropollutant.

That's why we teamed up with a biodegradable glitter company, BioGlitz. Now Project Unicorn isn't harming the environment, and it can't make anyone unhappy. Unless they just don't like glitter.

9
BE THE CHANGE

Project Unicorn helped me speak up about what it is like to have a disability. Some people think "disability" is a bad word, but for me, it has opened the doors to all kinds of new opportunities. I know that hasn't happened to everyone who is disabled. I also know that when some people see me, they automatically think I don't have abilities just because I don't have a hand. I realize my experience is the same as but different from so many other kids with a disability. That's why I told my mom that I wanted to keep speaking out and to help other kids have experiences like mine.

I just want to fit into a world that usually doesn't see a lot of pictures and videos of people who look different. When they do share pictures of people who are different, it's usually because that person happens to be good at something. Usually it's sports or acting or modeling. I want to live in a world where a person who may not have all of his or her limbs can do things well, and it doesn't have to be big news. Imagine if a limb-different actor or actress was on a TV show, and it was just a normal thing. Disabilities are everywhere in the world. It doesn't have to be a big focus every time in the media. People with disabilities can be treated like anyone else if the people who write and put together TV shows and movies just include them instead of making the disability the focus of a character.

Plus, there are other ways to be successful.

I think that's why my mom is trying so hard to encourage me to do things beyond sports and theater. Sports are a lot of fun, and I know it all makes me stronger. I love performing. But people who are disabled can become so many things. I'm finding ways to show how a limb-different person can get involved in STEAM (which means science, technology, engineering, arts, and math) and design. And who knows what else? The only thing that can stop us is our attitudes. My attitude is to just keep trying!

I kept trying with design after I came up with my first glitter-shooting idea. I didn't stop after that first camp. I kept learning every day. I couldn't have done that without the help of my parents and Sam. He would meet with me even on days when I just wanted to eat a snack and go have fun with my friends. All the adults who saw my interest spark after I created my first glitter cannon jumped in and really supported me. I want to help more kids get that opportunity.

Now that I have some design experience, I'm trying to take time to learn so much more. Along with getting the chance to get hands-on experience building my latest helper arm with Mr. David, I am starting to meet other types of designers. I was invited to a fashion innovation studio in New York City to see how a clothing company designs for a season. I met with fashion designers and got to share my thoughts. The grown-ups in the room let me give some different views on a collection of activewear. I never doubted myself when we talked about the clothes. I trust my opinions, and I love sharing my thoughts and ideas. I don't know if I would have been able to do that before I jumped into Project Unicorn.

Each conversation I have is a chance to change thoughts about disabilities.

PETITION FOR CHANGE

Have you ever owned a toy that looked like you? When I was four years old, my mom bought me an American Girl doll and gave me an outfit that matched the doll. She thought we looked really cute together. She mentioned how the doll and I matched, but I was confused. I thought I understood what "matching" meant, but my doll and I didn't match. She didn't have one hand like I do. I asked my mom why my doll didn't look like me, and she told me she hadn't thought of it that way. I had never seen a doll with a limb difference. I felt like I might never see a toy that matched me.

That experience turned into another big idea, which I hope will help kids understand differences a little better. Dolls are a key to making a change. I talked about this idea during one of my TEDx Talks. I think dolls are an important way for all kids to see disabilities in a different light. My T-shirts were another idea I had to use a simple message to get the word out about physical differences. I am trying really hard to make sure more people see limb differences out in the open so they won't need to whisper and stare the next time they see a kid who may not have hands or feet. There are so many kids and adults in this world who have disabilities. It shouldn't be something that's scary. Kids just need to understand disabilities more when they are little. That's why I started a petition to ask one of the biggest doll companies to consider offering limb-different dolls.

My petition is on a website called Change.org, and I made a video explaining how I love dolls, but I've always wanted to see a doll in toy stores that looks like me. If you have ever walked into an American Girl store, there are a bunch of displays of Truly Me dolls. They are supposed to look like you and me. The dolls come with outfits you can wear to match your doll. American Girl sells a lot of extra things to go with a doll so it can look more like its owner. There are glasses and earrings, crutches, wheelchairs, and even allergy-alert bracelets and insulin pumps.

One of the most obvious differences you will see with some of the American Girl dolls on display is that some of the dolls don't have hair. Those dolls are available for kids who are going through cancer treatments, which is super important. And they have expanded the line to be inclusive of different skin tones, which is also so important for representation. But none of the dolls sold by American Girl have limb differences. I'd love to have an American Girl doll look like me. But even more, I'd love for all the kids who walk into a store to look at the displays and see how some of the dolls wear a prosthetic leg or don't have a hand. Toys represent the world that we see every day. Why can't our dolls match reality? I think a lot of people agree with me, because the petition has more than twenty thousand signatures, and I don't plan to stop talking about it.

Since I started the petition, I had some opportunities to spread the word about what I think of American Girl dolls. I got to talk to some different journalists and even did a live online show with CBS. A story about my petition got onto the front page of the *Kansas City Star*! I just don't stop talking about it. I think that's why I've gotten so many signatures.

Not long after my petition started, a company in New York that makes prostheses started offering a free service to upgrade the dolls for free for any child who has a limb difference. Parents just have to send their dolls to the company, and it is returned wearing prostheses. My parents sent my Truly Me doll to get the upgrade, and it is so cool to finally have an American Girl doll that really does look like me.

About a year later the Vermont Teddy Bear Company made a big step forward for limb-difference toys when it started selling limb-difference options in April 2017. When you click to purchase a bear, you can pick the different type of limb differences. It is amazing to look at the order form online and see options like "left above elbow" (that's my type of limb difference) and "right below knee." People can order bears that match their bodies. When the bear arrives in the mail, it actually has smaller arms or legs! My three-pawed bear is really cute and has a sparkle skirt and bow.

American Girl hasn't made any changes yet, but I believe they are exploring how to make their line more inclusive, and I can't wait to see what is next.

American Girl is a part of the larger Mattel corporation, and I am very proud that I recently had a chance to work with a different part of the Mattel company. My work around speaking out about the importance of inclusive toys inspired the brand, and they invited me to talk to Barbie designers about limb differences and dolls. The initial doll idea we came up with didn't happen. But I learned that the design process doesn't always lead to something you find in toy stores. Not every idea turns into a doll that goes on sale.

But we kept working together, and I helped weigh in on a new doll with a prosthetic leg that is launching in 2019! I had a chance to give my thoughts about the design and look. I met with the Barbie team to share what it's like to be limb different and how I talk about my experience with disabilities. I am so excited to see stores around the world selling a doll that has a limb difference! It's my dream to see kids walking by a Barbie shelf and see a physical difference lined up with all the other dolls. I know they are on a journey to continue to evolve, and I know this will continue on to make the doll line more reflective of the world.

This isn't about me; it's about all the kids in this world who have physical differences. They deserve to see themselves in our toys. I want more kids to go to stores and see little arms and legs with or without prosthetics on the shelves. Kids with typical bodies will learn about limb differences before they see me or someone like me on a playground or in school for the first time. Maybe they won't sit down at a public table and stare intensely at a kid who looks different. Toys aren't just fun—they can educate kids on what we see in this world. Limb differences are real!

10
WE'RE ALL DIFFERENT

My normal is not your normal. We all have different thoughts and different experiences. Some are more obvious than others. While some people will want to use your difference as something that is bad, I think it's what makes you awesome. The trick is not letting other people try to change you just because you're different. Be proud of it!

I have a lot of friends who are "typical." But guess what? They all feel different. That's the strange thing about being a kid. I think I'm lucky to look different because I can't pretend I'm *not* different. Instead, I've learned to have fun with it. Yes, there are days when I'd rather not stand out in a crowd. But most days, I'm proud to be me. I think you can be proud too, especially if there are issues or topics that you really enjoy. You can use those things to help you speak up and maybe even help others.

HOW CAN YOU MAKE A DIFFERENCE?

Name Something That Makes You Different:

Activities You Love:

People/Places/Things That Matter to You:

Organizations You Have Joined:

Organizations You Want to Join:

Take a look at all your answers and ask yourself some questions, like "Do the organizations I have joined relate to the people/places/things that matter to me?"

Think about the times when you felt different. Is there a way you can use your activities or interests to help others understand why your difference is great?

Are there groups that help you connect with your difference? (You might be able to learn from others who understand!)

You can reach out to an adult in your life to help make these connections. My mom and dad made sure I got to meet other people with disabilities, and they made sure I could attend camps and other activities so I wouldn't feel alone.

Think about the answers you got from the quiz. Are you extra creative because of your difference? Maybe it helps you be braver. I think my difference taught me how to meet a ton of people who inspire my work to help change perceptions. What does the quiz say about you, and how can you use it to change the world for the better?

YOU CAN HELP TOO

If you go to school with someone with a disability, you can get to know that person. Introduce yourself. You will probably discover that he or she is a really cool human. Having a difference can make you pretty sarcastic and funny. I think I'm pretty funny, but I know I'm super sarcastic.

ADVICE FROM JORDAN

Dear Jordan: How do I start a conversation with someone who has a disability? I don't want to seem rude!

A: I really think it's important to say hello. Do not ask the person what is "wrong" with them. Just introduce yourself. Let that person know you were interested in knowing them and wanted to say hi. You will quickly find out if this person is interested in talking or not. Most of the time, if I meet someone who is curious and respectful, I'll tell them about my little arm.

Dear Jordan: If someone looks different, it's really hard not to stare. Should I look away?

A: I really, really don't like staring. But I also really don't like people who avoid me because they seem scared about my difference. Instead of looking away, look that person in the eye and say hello. Then it's okay to keep moving. It's not cool to stop and watch that person. Treat them like a regular person because they *are* a regular person. Accept that that person looks different and move on. Not everyone looks like you. That's the real world.

Dear Jordan: What can I do to help people with disabilities if I don't have one?

A: Don't feel sorry for people with disabilities. If you hear someone making fun of a person or feeling sad about a person's way of life because she is disabled, speak up. Let them know a disability is not sad. It might be hard. That person might need a lot of help to live. But all people deserve to be treated with kindness. All people deserve to be treated like you would like to be treated: with respect. People do not "suffer from" a disability. They *live* with a disability. A person who uses a wheelchair is not "wheelchair-bound." A wheelchair is freedom. They are a wheelchair user. Shift how you think about disability, and let your friends and family know when you hear conversations that go against your new knowledge.

Dear Jordan: What are other ways I can support the disability community?

A: If you are making decisions, don't forget to include people with disabilities. That might be hard if you don't know someone with a disability. Find the groups in your town that support disability. Ask those organizations if there are health support groups or clubs where people with disabilities hang out and work together. Search Twitter and see if there are people with disabilities in your area sharing input online. Social media helps connect people with disabilities who might have a hard time leaving the house. It also helps people with similar differences find one another so they can learn and share together.

HOW CAN YOU CHANGE THE WORLD?

I believe I can change the world, and you can too! Do you have a perspective or difference that others may not understand? Here are steps I think you can take to move from having a big idea to getting more people to talk about it.

SPEAK UP AND DON'T STOP

I can't hide my difference. So why not talk about it? Most of the time, I'd rather talk about my difference than pretend it's not there. When I see someone super confused about my difference, I like to offer information. If someone is being rude about my difference, I usually let it slide, or I have a friend around to help me out. Having a glitter superpower helped me talk about limb differences more than usual. A purple unicorn horn that shoots sparkles is even more unusual than a little arm.

SHARE YOUR THOUGHTS IN AS MANY WAYS AS YOU CAN

I'm lucky my mom had a blog when I started speaking up about disabilities. She was able to share the fun I was having. When I started getting the chance to speak to journalists, I was excited to share how the combination of disability and design leads to really fun things.

TEAM UP WITH OTHERS TO GET THE WORD OUT

Some of the kids who have gotten to know Born Just Right, which you'll learn more about in the next chapter, are now helping raise money for the organization. They're sharing information about our nonprofit and talking about how it can be fun being different. Even adults, with and without disabilities, have volunteered to share information at expo tables or pass out brochures at events.

BE YOURSELF!

You are the only you that is out there in this world. Just trusting your thoughts and sharing them can make a difference. It's really that simple. You might help one person, and you might help a million. It doesn't really matter as long as you're helping.

11
BORN JUST RIGHT FOUNDATION

My superhero experience continues to spread across the country and around the world. I've seen articles online about my invention in all kinds of different languages. I've even had invites to speak in other countries. All these opportunities came out of a chance to enjoy the body I have with pride. I don't plan on Project Unicorn being the only thing I invent. I feel like I'm just getting started. Now that I've learned how strong I feel by solving my own design needs, I want to help other kids do the same. Thanks to my experiences, my mom and

I launched a new nonprofit organization and named it after the online community we've grown through the years—Born Just Right. It is a site that started out as a blog my mom used to tell my story. We started meetups when I traveled and grew a community on Facebook. When my Project Unicorn work got bigger, I told my mom I wanted to try to use the awesome and positive feedback we were receiving to help our message reach as many people as possible. And Born Just Right has helped us do just that.

My hope is to use Born Just Right to help more kids use disability as a way to learn their strengths. Each one of us has different challenges and ideas. What if we all learned how to take our differences to create something exciting instead of thinking our differences are something bad? Born Just Right is teaming up with other organizations to create more design lessons for kids with disabilities. I hope we can work with companies that want to hear different views on what works with their products. If Born Just Right can help a whole bunch of kids discover their inner designer, then those kids can work with all kinds of different businesses or groups. We would be able to talk about anything! We could help car designers build different designs. Maybe we could help clothing lines add extra-stretchy clothes or designs that are comfortable in a new way. From medical tools to clothing to fun toys, I think kids like me have views that no one else has considered.

While we grow the nonprofit, my mom and I are trying to continue to talk and teach about how disabilities are not a sad thing. Disabilities are a part of everyone's world. We are a group of people who should not be ignored. Instead of looking at disabilities as a bad thing, let's find ways to use them to our advantage. I know having a disability changes how I see the world, and I am a better person for that view. By speaking up, I use that view to hopefully change thoughts on limb differences and disabilities. Maybe I helped change views on prosthetics. When you build an "arm," it doesn't have to look real. It can be anything. It can be a unicorn horn that shoots sparkles, or it can be an arm that helps you play the violin. People who don't have a hand don't need a "hand." We need helpful and fun tools.

GROWING BORN JUST RIGHT

One quiet summer day in Boston, a group of kids gathered in an open conference room of a shared working space. It was the first time our nonprofit worked on a daylong design event for kids with limb differences. We had kids with upper and lower differences join us for a day of fun and creativity. I was so excited to put together a new event for kids!

I got to join the kids in brainstorming and coming up with new ideas to turn themselves into superheroes. In the meantime, my mom gathered all the parents in a separate room to talk about how they can all support kids in STEAM and design.

The kids in our group had so many fun ideas. We spent the morning brainstorming and the afternoon building out concepts. I came up with a new way to surprise people with glitter—a prosthetic arm that throws balls that explode with glitter when they land. (It's really messy.) One girl developed LED lights for her helper legs. Another built a Wonder Woman shield for her little arm. There was a marshmallow shooter, a pool-noodle battle arm, a helpful arm table, a hands-free book holder, and a useful tool for one girl to do her metal artwork. We all presented our designs to the parents. It was awesome to see so many great ideas in such a short time.

We put together longer events for kids since then, and we've given our workshop a new name: BOOST by Born Just Right. Some of the workshop participants continue to work on improving their prototypes with design buddies. I am so excited to see what new ideas come next.

Along with setting up awesome events for kids, my mom and I had a chance to speak and share about Born Just Right with all kinds of really cool organizations. We've spoken at the national AIGA Design Conference (a professional organization for design), the South by Southwest Interactive Festival (a massive film, interactive media, and music festival), and even the United State of Women Summit. We are just getting started!

12
DESIGN YOUR DREAMS

I'm surrounded by so many family members, friends, and teachers who support me. It's given me the freedom to explore and try all kinds of life experiences that may not happen for everyone in their lifetimes. That's probably why so many people ask me about what I want to do when I grow up. I usually just say that I know I want to go to college.

I don't think I'm ready to commit to a specific career, but I'm starting to get an idea of what I really enjoy and what can make an impact in this world. I know I want to keep using design for good. I got to meet members of MIT's Little Devices Lab, and I've learned how tinkering with small things can create big changes in the medical industry. The lab is creating makerspaces in hospitals for nurses and doctors to create solutions to tiny problems. They also invent low-tech tools to help people in third-world countries. I've even seen simple ideas that can help save thousands and thousands of dollars in hospitals.

I had a chance to meet designers of products and clothing. I have learned that thinking about disability or "inclusive design" isn't always a part of the design process. Many industries are just starting to change that. I would love to use my input for good in so many different parts of design.

I love the chance to help teach other kids and adults about design. In the last couple of years, I got to speak to adults at a lot of events to help them learn how to let kids lead their own design ideas. I want kids with disabilities to have a say in the products they need and the ones that would just make their lives more fun. I don't think there's a degree in college that is about changing perspectives, but maybe I can create one! What I know is that we are all different, and our differences can help us all make a better world with design or whatever topic or issue that excites us.

LAUNCHING YOUR OWN DREAMS

I keep mentioning all the talks I'm giving to adults. Why do I have to just talk to adults? I want to share some of my lessons with YOU. Maybe it can help change the way you think about disability, or just about the power we all have as kids. I know a lot of you have great ideas, and you shouldn't be afraid to act on them!

YOUR IDEAS MATTER

If you have a good idea, don't bury it. See if you have an adult in your life who can help you take that idea and make it bigger. If that isn't possible, write down your idea, draw it, or do whatever you can not to forget. And do your best to make that idea come true. Maybe it's just talking about it to your friends. And when you get more comfortable, share it with other people you know—maybe a teacher you trust. If you think you can make a difference, you can! I have the chance to talk to adults, and I keep telling them to listen to kids! We have really great ideas.

TAKE TIME TO BE CREATIVE

Thinking up ideas and creating things takes time. You have to give yourself a little time each week to step away from technology and draw or write down thoughts.

FAILURE ALWAYS HAPPENS

Keep working and don't give up. If you believe in your ideas, you will find a solution. Some of my best prototypes came out of previous models that weren't working right, and it gave us the tools to learn what wasn't working. If you create something without failure, you probably need to keep working on it to make it better.

I have my moments of doubt. Don't we all? But I think having moments of failure helps remind me to move past that doubt. I know I can keep going. How can I learn anything without making mistakes? Give yourself a break and keep learning. Growing ideas takes time. I don't know if I will ever be totally happy with the Project Unicorn design. Sam and I have worked on it for more than two years! Your best idea may not happen immediately. It may not even happen while you're a kid. If you are confident in solving a problem, just keep trying.

WHAT'S NEXT?

My life experiences have combined into a magical adventure. All the glitter and excitement came from believing in myself and having an amazing group of people in my life who believe in me too.

What's next? I am going to keep speaking about disabilities and design. I hope my work will make sure more businesses think about inclusive design and bring in people with disabilities to share their thoughts and ideas. I hope more kids with disabilities can get a chance to learn how to talk about their design needs and make those ideas come to life. I am not the only person with a disability trying to change what typical people understand when they see someone with a different body or different abilities. One day, I would like to see a person judged for his or her knowledge and not from a snap decision just because that person has a different-looking body.

It is going to take all of us to learn more about disabilities. It is going to take all of us to get to know and talk to people who don't look like us. My mom and I made a pact that we would work together to help as many people who are different as we can. That's why we are working so hard to grow Born Just Right as a nonprofit. We can all find our own ways to respect disabilities. Many times, it just starts with a conversation, maybe even a hello when you pass by someone who has a physical difference.

When I was little, my parents would read all kinds of picture books that talk about our differences. Books where one kid has red hair, one kid has glasses, one kid uses crutches . . . We are all different. Instead of feeling scared when you are with someone who doesn't look or act like you, give that person a chance. Learn from them!

I think we can all learn a lot more when we talk to one another about our differences. That's when we learn new things, and maybe that will help us all create more great and fun ideas. If not, at least we will all understand one another more! At the end of the day, we are all born just right.

SITES YOU SHOULD KNOW ABOUT

Born Just Right: The nonprofit run by Jordan and her mom, Jen
bornjustright.org

STEAM Squad: Jordan and her STEAM friends
thesteamsquad.org

MAKE magazine: A community of makers around the world
makezine.com

Tinkercad: The first 3-D CAD tool Jordan used
tinkercad.com

Girls Who Code: A nonprofit that aims to support and increase the number of women in computer science
girlswhocode.com

DIY: A site that awards kids with digital (and real, if you want to pay) badges for making stuff
diy.org

Eighteenx18: A creative platform to engage the young generation to speak our truth, get active, and (once you're old enough) vote!
eighteenx18.com

Black Girls Code: A nonprofit that focuses on providing technology education for African-American girls
blackgirlscode.com

Être: A resource site where motivated girls can find the tools they need.
etregirls.com

GenderAvenger: An organization focused on making sure women (and girls) are included in public events
genderavenger.com

Girls on the Run: Jordan enjoyed running and learning about girl power through this organization.
girlsontherun.org

ACKNOWLEDGMENTS

Books don't appear magically. It takes a lot of time and support from many people. First and foremost, we need to thank Randy (Dad) and Cam. Your support and love make everything we do possible. We are so lucky you both support us when we're home and when we're away. Our family is unusual for our experiences near and far, but you both keep us grounded. We love you so much.

There are other family members who are so important to us. Lots of love to Uncle Barry and Aunt Jenn, Colin, Camden, Addison, Grandma and Grandpa Lee, Poppy and Ruth Ann, Uncle Jon and Grant. Thank you for the love and guidance you've all given us.

Huge shout-outs to our literary agent, John Cusick, and our incredible editor, Alyson Heller. We stumbled into the most perfect team to help us learn about the vast world of publishing. We appreciate the time and attention you've given us to navigate this experience.

There aren't enough sheets of paper in the world to be able to include each and every person who has made an impact on our lives. First, we want to thank our local community of friends. Jordan is so thankful for her friends in and outside of her school, but especially Quin and Reese. Jen is amazed by the network of women and men who are there to listen and make sure we meet other changemakers in the area. Unplanned text messages that lead to our gatherings are the very best. We are also very lucky to have Alex George from Skylark Books as a friend and guide through the book publishing process.

We are connected to so many amazing current and past students, faculty, and staff at the University of Missouri. We have been a part of the Mizzou community in many different ways. From the medical community, the journalism school, and the staff of the Joint Office of Strategic Communications and Marketing, we are obviously Mizzou Made. We have to give an extra thank-you to the many Mizzou alumni who work in newsrooms everywhere and have helped us tell the Born Just Right story.

Big thanks to our friends who live across the country: bloggers, progressive activists, digital marketing experts, and even our amazing family from the Disney Parks Moms Panel. They have all helped us along the way. It's stunning how many people play a special role in our lives.

There are many different people who have made a special impact in our lives through the disability community. Thank you to Liz Jackson, Nikki Kelly, Angel Giuffria, Rebekah Marine, Mary Leighton and Camp No Limits, all of our friends at Wounded Warrior Amputee Softball Team (especially Nick Clark), Amputee Coalition of America's Amp Camp, Helping Hands Foundation, and our Sammy's Friends from long, long ago. Ryan Haack, you and your family are something special. (Eric and Patti, your families fall in the same category.)

Thanks to the amazing people who keep Born Just Right, the nonprofit, up and running with us. Thank you to Born Just Right's Design Director Sam Hobish and Senior Programming Director

Kate Ganim, along with board members Sarah Granger, Chuck Donalies, and Nicole Shea. We're also thankful to Sarah O'Rourke at Autodesk for her long-term support of Jordan and Born Just Right's work. Thank you, Ellen Gerstein, for not only your friendship but your insight and guidance for BJR. Thanks to Dave ("Mr. David") Rotter for your support as an advisor to Born Just Right *and* Jordan's evolution as a prosthetic wearer and designer.

There are some special DC folks we want to make sure we include:

Sara and Giff, thank you for your constant love and the chance to be a part of our lives when we are near and far away. Jen looks forward to future happy hours in person or over Google Hangouts. She is not picky. Heidi and Chuck, we are so lucky you have offered your time and friendship in so many ways. Your family has a special place in our hearts. Stef and Marlene, we are just getting started. We hope our adventures continue together.

Thanks to Jordan's growing STEAM Squad (especially cofounders Julie Sage, Taylor Richardson, and Allie Weber), #YoungScientistProbs, and #WeVoteNext friends. You are rock stars and we're honored to be connected with you and your parents.

Finally, thank you to the Born Just Right community—the families, kids, and adults who have connected with us through the years. Thank you for going on this journey with us. We can't wait to see what we all create next together.

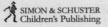